CONTENTS

Acknowledgements

The author would like to thank Bruce Lorimer, BSc, Dip TP, MRTPI; Julie Grover; and the staff of the Official Publications Room, Cambridge University Library, for their help in the preparation of this book.

The author and publishers wish to thank the following who have kindly given permission for the use of copyright material:

Associated Book Publishers (UK) Ltd for an extract from 'The Meaning of Poverty' by Peter Townsend, *British Journal of Sociology*, October 1962; John Farquharson Ltd on behalf of the Tom Harrisson Mass Observation Archive for extracts from *Living Through the Blitz* by Tom Harrisson, 1976, *Meet Yourself at the Doctor's*, 1949 and *War begins at Home*, 1940 by Tom Harrisson and Charles Madge; The Controller of Her Majesty's Stationery Office for Crown copyright material; *The Independent* for an extract from 'Survivors on the welfare estate' by Jeremy Seabrook, 17.1.87; *The Listener* for extracts from 'Memoirs of the Unemployed', 2.8.33 and 9.8.33; The Joseph Rowntree Charitable Trust for extracts from *Poverty: A Study of Town Life* by Seebohm Rowntree, 1900; Solo Syndication and Literary Agency Ltd on behalf of Mail Newspapers plc. for an extract from the *Daily Mail*, 5.7.48; Times Newspapers Ltd. for extracts from *The Times*, 5.7.48, 'How fares the brave new town?' by Brian James, *The Times*, 13.3.87 and 'Harlow 30 years after: how the dream stands up to reality' by Roger Berthoud, *The Times*, 16.12.77.

The author and publishers wish to acknowledge, with thanks, the following photographic sources:

BBC Hulton Picture Library pp 5, 13–14, 15, 23, 27 top, 27 bottom, 33, 34, 41 right, 45, 48 bottom, 57, 60 left; the Syndics of Cambridge University Library pp 11, 18, 19, 29 top, 38 top, 48 top, 49, 50, 51, 52–3; Camera Press pp 61, 62 top, 62 bottom; *Daily Mail* pp 38 bottom, 43; *Illustrated London News* p 13 top; Imperial War Museum pp 17, 36; *The Independent* p 63 bottom; John Topham Picture Library pp 7, 25, 29 bottom, 30 top, 30 bottom, 31, 39, 41 left, 52 left, 52 right, 52–3, 55, 60 right, 63 top.

Every effort has been made to trace all the copyright holders, but if any have been inadvertently overlooked, the publishers will be pleased to make the necessary arrangements at the first opportunity.

Cover illustration: *The Food Queue*, 1917, by C.R.W. Nevinson. Reproduced by courtesy of the Imperial War Museum.

PREFACE

The study of history is exciting, whether in a good story well told, a mystery solved by the judicious unravelling of clues, or a study of the men, women and children whose fears and ambitions, successes and tragedies make up the collective memory of mankind.

This series aims to reveal this excitement to pupils through a set of topic books on important historical subjects from the Middle Ages to the present day. Each book contains four main elements: a narrative and descriptive text, lively and relevant illustrations, extracts of contemporary evidence, and questions for further thought and work. Involvement in these elements should provide an adventure which will bring the past to life in the imagination of the pupil.

Each book is also designed to develop the knowledge, skills and concepts so essential to a pupil's growth. It provides a wide, varying introduction to the evidence available on each topic. In handling this evidence, pupils will increase their understanding of basic historical concepts such as causation and change, as well as of more advanced ideas such as revolution and democracy. In addition, their use of basic study skills will be complemented by more sophisticated historical skills such as the detection of bias and the formulation of opinion.

The intended audience for the series is pupils of eleven to sixteen years; it is expected that the earlier topics will be introduced in the first three years of secondary school, while the nineteenth and twentieth century topics are directed towards first examinations.

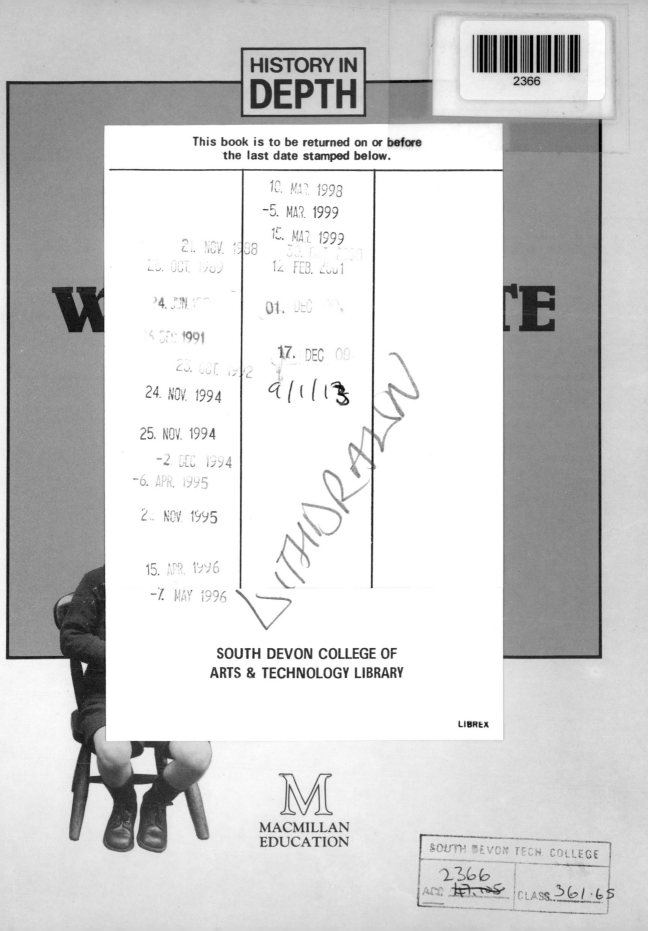

HISTORY IN
DEPTH

M
MACMILLAN
EDUCATION

For Marina

First published 1988

Published by
MACMILLAN EDUCATION LTD
Houndmills, Basingstoke, Hampshire RG21 2XS
and London
Companies and representatives
throughout the world

Printed in Hong Kong

British Library Cataloguing in Publication Data
Sillars, Stuart
The welfare state.——(History in depth).
1. Welfare state——History   2. Public
welfare——Great Britain——History——20th
century
I. Title   II. Series
361.6'5'0941   HV245
ISBN 0–333–43838–8

PRINCIPLES AND FOUNDATIONS

The year is 1900. Against the advice of his friends, an American novelist sets out in a hansom cab to see for himself what living conditions are like in the East End of London.

> *Nowhere in the streets of London may one escape the sight of abject poverty, while five minutes' walk from almost any point will bring one to a slum; but the region my hansom was now penetrating was one unending slum. The streets were filled with a new and different race of people, short of stature, and of wretched or beer-sodden appearance. We rolled along through miles of bricks and squalor, and from each cross street and alley flashed long vistas of bricks and misery. Here and there lurched a drunken man or woman, and the air was obscene with sounds of jangling and squabbling. At a market, tottery old men were searching in the garbage thrown in the mud for rotten potatoes, beans and vegetables, while little children clustered like flies around a festering mass of fruit, thrusting their arms to the shoulders into the liquid corruption, and drawing forth morsels but partially decayed, which they devoured on the spot.*
>
> Jack London: *The People of the Abyss*, 1903

Terraced houses in the East End of London in the 1900s

Why did conditions such as these exist in one of the richest, most powerful nations in the world? It is not easy to answer this question – but in the early years of this century it was one that was being asked increasingly often. To answer it we must understand the attitudes of the government and people of the time. First, however, we need to know how the nation provided for its poorer citizens at the time when Jack London was writing.

Many of the people London wrote about had jobs. They worked in the docks, in factories or as labourers in the City and East End, but wages were low and there was no security of employment. Men could be put out of work with no warning and they and their families – which were often large as contraception was not generally used – had to survive as well as they could. There was no state unemployment benefit.

For those with no money there was 'relief' under the Poor Law, paid for out of the local rates and administered by Poor Law Guardians. Accepting relief usually meant living in a workhouse, an institution where men and women were given hard work to do in return for meagre meals and shelter. Workhouses bore a sense of disgrace, deliberately created to prevent people from taking advantage of the system, and they were often run by people who felt that the poor were responsible for their own misfortune. Paupers in workhouses were deprived of the right to vote and families were split up, so people did everything in their power to stay out of them.

In some areas there was a system of 'outdoor relief', in which poor people were given money in return for work and were allowed to stay in their own homes. Elsewhere there was no such scheme, and the workhouse was often the only hope for the destitute. Charities offered some help, guided by the Charity Organisation Society, a body set up in 1869 to decide exactly what charities could do, and to help them do it. But many people were reluctant to ask their assistance, seeing charity as a handout from the wealthy.

A 'two-up, two-down' early Victorian terraced house, run down and quite inadequate for its tenants by 1900

A rural slum

The living conditions of most poor people at this time were appalling. Every city had its slum areas. A flurry of Acts of Parliament in the late nineteenth century had given local Medical Officers of Health powers to supply sanitation and clear slums, and in some places such as Birmingham this was done. But local authorities were only empowered, not compelled, to demolish slums, and other cities took little or no action.

It was not only in cities that housing was poor. Farm workers often lived in derelict cottages made of cob – mud and straw – with thatched roofs which were rotten and verminous.

In such conditions disease was rife. Although cholera had been halted in the nineteenth century, there were other killer diseases. Insanitary conditions bred typhus fever, and poor ventilation and factory smoke encouraged tuberculosis – the dreaded consumption which killed 70–80 000 people every year. Scarlet fever and measles – now easily controlled – were killers. We can begin to understand the state of health of the poor if we think of conditions today in many Third World countries.

Some advances had been made, however. In 1853 vaccination against smallpox was made compulsory and was carried out by Poor Law Medical Officers. As everyone was treated, not just paupers, this did a little to remove the disgrace of contact with the Poor Law, and a great deal towards stamping out the disease. But apart from this, there was no scheme for medical treatment. Doctors had to be paid for each visit and, as a result, few of the poor consulted them. Some doctors helped their poor patients by 'Robin Hood medicine' – charging their wealthy clients more, to cover the cost of treating the needy – but in some areas there were no wealthy patients. Although hospitals were run by charities, most poor people were taken to Poor Law infirmaries, set up by the Guardians but kept separate from the workhouses.

Conversion Chart
6d. = 2½p
1s. = 5p
2s. = 10p
5s. = 25p
10s. = 50p
15s. = 75p
20s. = £1

Many working men made provision for sickness through trade unions or friendly societies:

The Dunmow Society was one of the most wonderful thrift organisations ever erected.... The organisation was by parishes, generally through the parson, and cost almost nothing. For 6d. a member got a death benefit, medical benefit, sickness and disablement, and a small pension. The Society was solvent and quite a large proportion of the badly-paid Suffolk labourers were in it.

William Braithwaite: *Lloyd George's Ambulance Wagon*, 1957

Friendly societies gave some measure of security to working men and their families against sickness and the cost of burial — for the 'death benefit' mentioned here was paid to cover funeral expenses and thus avoid a 'pauper's funeral', the final disgrace which working people did all they could to avoid. Yet 6d. a week was a lot to pay, when a farm worker in Suffolk earned only about 10s. a week. Many working men could not keep up the contributions, faced with a choice between paying them and buying food for the family.

For the poorly paid, the unemployed and the elderly there was little security in the early 1900s. What aid there was came from a bewildering range of sources: the Poor Law Guardians, the Medical Officer of Health, the Poor Law Medical Officer, the charities and the friendly societies. For the old, who had been unable to keep up payments to a friendly society, there was nothing except the workhouse. As well as being inadequate, the system for helping the poor was totally confused. It was all a very long way from our idea of a welfare state.

Questions

1 What do you think are the strengths and weaknesses of the passage by Jack London, in terms of showing the conditions in which the poor lived? For the historian, does the fact that London was a novelist affect the value of the passage?

2 Copy out and complete the chart below, listing all the different kinds of help available to the poor in the early 1900s.

Organisation	Help offered	How financed
Friendly societies	Insurance against sickness; burial expenses; pension.	Weekly contribution from worker.

What is the welfare state?

In 1942 — three years after the beginning of World War II — a government report appeared which outlined the idea of what we now call the welfare state. Its basis was 'social insurance' — insurance by the state against unemployment and sickness, and regular allowances paid to parents with young children. At this time (as later chapters will show) there was some provision for those in need, but each type of aid was covered by a different body — there were just as many as there had been in 1900, but they were not the same organisations. The author of the report, Sir William Beveridge, wanted to improve these services and bring them all under a single organisation. To suggest such a scheme in wartime was a bold step, but Beveridge thought that the fighting was in itself a strong reason for change:

Now, when the war is abolishing landmarks of every kind, is the opportunity for using experience in a clear field. A revolutionary movement in the world's history is a time for revolutions, not for patching. . . . Organisation of social insurance should be treated as one part only of social progress. Social insurance fully developed may provide income security; it is an attack upon Want. But Want is one only of five giants on the road of reconstruction and in some ways the easiest to attack. The others are Disease, Ignorance, Squalor and Idleness.

William Beveridge: *Social Insurance and Allied Services*, 1942

A popular paper's explanation of the Beveridge plan. How many organisations does John Jones have to deal with?

Picture Post, March 6, 1943

WHAT A MINISTRY OF SOCIAL SECURITY WOULD MEAN TO THE ORDINARY CITIZEN

What happens to-day to an individual who meets with misfortune : an extreme case to illustrate the maze through which Beveridge has pointed out a clear, simple way.

1 John Jones, a man of 64, finds that he has fallen out of work through no fault of his own.

2 He draws unemployment pay : at this point his case is dealt with by the Ministry of Labour.

3 After 26 weeks he is no longer entitled to the dole and is turned away to go elsewhere.

4 He has now to go to the Assistance Board. Here he applies for the unemployment help he needs.

5 The first of many investigators arrives at his home—this time from the Assistance Board.

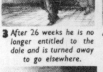

6 He falls ill. Unable to work, he is no longer able to get help from the Assistance Board.

7 A new investigator arrives—from the Approved Society, which now deals with his case.

8 Still another investigator —from the local Public Assistance Committee, to which he has had to apply.

9 His 65th birthday present: a visit from a fourth investigator — to look into his pension claim

Wife Falls Ill

Son Steals

MEANWHILE

Child Is Ill

All Mean More Investigators

A MINISTRY OF SOCIAL SECURITY WOULD COMBINE ALL THESE FUNCTIONS

John Jones when he falls out of work has plenty of trouble besides the gnawing anxiety about his family's welfare. He is passed from one set of officials to another until he feels like an official form worn out by constant stamping. How absurd that a fresh investigation has to worry him whenever he suffers a new misfortune, that there is no single set of papers about him and his family for everybody to consult! When he comes to the end of his road—an old age pension—

he reaches the crowning absurdity: at this point his case actually comes under Customs and Excise! It is this state of affairs which a Ministry of Social Security would cure. John Jones would go to one local office for all his claims; there would be one set of papers about him and one investigator to help and advise. And the people working in this office would not treat him as a wrong-doer, but as a man fallen on evil times who must be lifted up again.

Beveridge's plan was only a suggestion. In the late 1940s, Clement Attlee's Labour Government adopted some, but not all, of its proposals (see Chapter 4). But the report did establish that the state was responsible for providing a united system, to prevent the return of the kind of living conditions described by Jack London.

The modern welfare state can be defined like this: the provision by the state of housing, education, a complete range of medical services (doctors, dentists, eye treatment and hospitals), unemployment payments, help with finding work, and a range of other benefits such as maternity, child and funeral allowances and financial aid for those in need, such as the old, the unemployed and the sick.

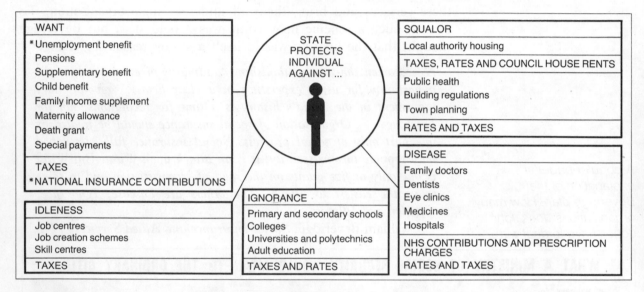

WANT	STATE PROTECTS INDIVIDUAL AGAINST ...	SQUALOR
*Unemployment benefit Pensions Supplementary benefit Child benefit Family income supplement Maternity allowance Death grant Special payments		Local authority housing
		TAXES, RATES AND COUNCIL HOUSE RENTS
		Public health Building regulations Town planning
		RATES AND TAXES
TAXES *NATIONAL INSURANCE CONTRIBUTIONS		DISEASE
		Family doctors Dentists Eye clinics Medicines Hospitals
IDLENESS	IGNORANCE	
Job centres Job creation schemes Skill centres	Primary and secondary schools Colleges Universities and polytechnics Adult education	NHS CONTRIBUTIONS AND PRESCRIPTION CHARGES
TAXES	TAXES AND RATES	RATES AND TAXES

The welfare state: how Beveridge's 'five giants' are attacked in the late 1980s and how the 'attacks' are funded

Since the years before World War I, politicians and social reformers have grappled with the problem of how these services should be provided. Should they be paid for out of taxes? Should they be withheld from people who have savings of their own?

These questions have an important bearing on the growth of the welfare state, and the way it is run now. Some services, such as public housing provided by local councils, are funded by rates and taxes, and by the rent paid by the people who live in the council houses. Other services, such as medical treatment and unemployment benefit, are contributory, which means that they are partly funded by regular contributions paid by each working person. Paying for the welfare state is a subject of passionate debate, and a single, unified system of welfare is still a long way off. Despite this, things have changed a great deal since 1900, as the rest of this book will show.

At the turn of the century a new approach was introduced: factual, scientific research into how much money the poor had, how they spent it, and the conditions in which they lived. Charles Booth in London and B. Seebohm Rowntree in York were the first to study the problem using the methods of the modern sociologist.

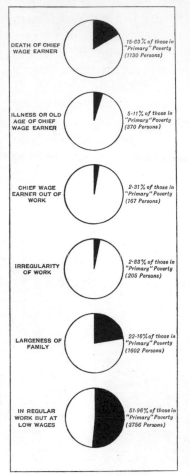

Rowntree hired 'investigators' to visit every house in 388 streets in York. In all, 46 754 people were included, making up about two-thirds of the city's population — a proportion far higher than that of most modern surveys. The results were published in a book called *Poverty*, which included detailed accounts of family budgets and a chapter on the dietary needs of working people, to explain that money was not wasted but was spent on basic necessities. Much of the book described living conditions, as in the following extract:

House No 6. Two rooms. In the lower one the brick floor is in holes. Fireplace without grate in bottom. Wooden floor of upper room has holes admitting numbers of mice. Roof very defective, the rain falling through on to the bed in wet weather. Outside wall also very damp, plaster falling off. Tenants apparently clean.

Courtyard. Houses all back-to-back. Yard cobbled and filthy. Ashpit overflowing. Water-supply for twelve houses from one tap placed in wall of privy.

B. Seebohm Rowntree: *Poverty: A Study of Town Life*, 1900

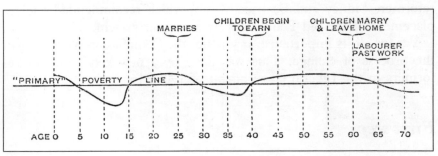

Rowntree was the first to illustrate his findings with charts and graphs.
Above left: the causes of 'primary' poverty, where earnings did not cover basic needs. Which are the most common?
Above right: times when a labourer is most likely to be poor. At what ages is poverty worst? Why?
Right: a page from one of Rowntree's investigators' notebooks. The average family income for those in work was 10s. 11d.; if the chief wage earner had died it was 8s. 7d., and if he was ill or too old to work it was 5s. 7d.

Questions

1 Rowntree's writing is simple and factual. How does it compare with Jack London's style of writing (page 5)? Which of the two do you think makes the slums more real? Which would make people want to change things, and why?

2 Study the extract from Rowntree's survey.
   a) How many people, on average, share a tap — the only source of water for washing and cooking?
   b) What does the information suggest about the role of women in households of this sort?

The work of Booth and Rowntree was one reason why a Royal Commission on the Poor Laws and the Relief of Distress was set up in 1905. Its main report, in 1909, said that the Poor Law should be reformed to meet individual needs and to help people to be independent. There was also a Minority Report, mainly written by the reformers Sidney and Beatrice Webb, which recommended the replacement of the old Poor Laws by a simpler system.

Yet for all its importance, it was not the Commission which began the process of change. This was done by a new generation of reformers in the Liberal Government of 1906–16.

First steps

In 1906, the Liberal Party won a general election with a large majority. However, there were a significant number of MPs from the new Labour Party (formed in 1900) in the House of Commons — a sign that the voice of the working people was at last beginning to be heard. Partly through fear of losing support to the new party, and partly through genuine concern, many members of the Liberal Party began to agree that there was a need for social reform. In 1906 the government supported a Labour Bill to provide free school meals for needy children, and this became the Education (Provision of Meals) Act. The following year a scheme for school medical inspections was introduced, and the Children Act of 1908 made neglect of a child by its parents a criminal offence. These were not dominant features of Liberal policy, and won government support grudgingly, but they were important reforms in their own right and paved the way for bolder steps.

The first of these was the Old Age Pensions Act of 1908. A pension of 5s. a week was paid to men and women over 70, and lower amounts were paid to those who earned between 8s. and 12s. a week. It was non-contributory, the money coming from the government's revenue from taxes.

How The Illustrated London News *reported the payment of state pensions, January 1909*

A demonstration against unemployment, 1908

The Bill met with much opposition. Lord Rosebery called it 'a mortal blow to the Empire', and Lord Lansdowne claimed that it would 'weaken the moral fibre of the nation, and diminish the self-respect of our people'. These objections were based on the idea of *laissez-faire*, a popular philosophy which meant leaving people to look after themselves. Despite the objections, pensions were introduced. They were completely independent of the Poor Law and so, for the first time, people became entitled to government aid without the disgrace of being paupers.

The first pensions were paid on 1 January 1909. Well over half a million people queued at post offices with their brightly coloured pension books — blue for those who were to receive the full 5s., cream for those who were to receive 4s., and so on down to the brick-red 1s. books. Altogether £119 166 13s. 4d. was paid out.

The pension made great changes in the lives of those receiving it. A popular newspaper interviewed one such couple, 'Darby, 72, with a cataract in one eye and very little sight in the other, Joan 71 last October'. They had lived on money given to them by their son and the meagre earnings from Joan's cleaning or 'charring' work:

Darby chuckled and said, 'It isn't wealth — no, you can't call it wealth — but it's something for sure.' They gave me their weekly budget at 10s. a week:

Coal (1 cwt)	1	6
Bread (3½ loaves)	1	4½
Butter (½lb)	0	6
Tea (6 oz)	0	6
Sugar (2lbs)	0	8
Milk (½d. per day)	0	3½
Soap	0	2
Gas	0	7
Firewood	0	2
Candles	0	1
Meat (on Sundays, lasting 3 days)	2	0
Half cowheel	0	5
Leaving towards occasional losses on sub-letting and lodgers, and for clothes	1	9

'You prefer that to going to the------?' I asked, hesitating to say the word 'Workhouse'.

'To The Other? said Joan quickly and with a look of terror. 'We'd sooner die here of starvation on the cold floor than that.'

Tears filled her old eyes as she mumbled, 'Three years we've struggled, but we've never been on the parish and we've never owed. We were very low, for you can't do much on 4s. a week, but we'd have died before we'd gone There.'

'The pension's not charity, it's a right,' Darby said proudly.

Daily Express, 2 January 1909

Questions

1 What is the reporter's attitude towards Darby and Joan? Bearing in mind the fact that the article appeared in a large-circulation newspaper, do you think this attitude was common? Explain your reasons carefully.

2 What is Darby and Joan's attitude to the workhouse and to charity? Does this suggest a reason why reforms were introduced quite separately from the Poor Law?

3 Do you think Darby and Joan are better or worse off than the households in Rowntree's survey? Give reasons for your answer.

Insuring the workers

necessary supplement thereto: something extra that is needed

Insurance against unemployment...stands in the closest relation to the organisation of the labour market, and forms the second line of attack on the problem of unemployment. It is, indeed, the necessary supplement thereto. The Labour Exchange is required to reduce to a minimum the intervals between successive jobs. Insurance is required to tide over the intervals that will still remain.... No plan other than insurance...is really adequate.

William Beveridge: *Unemployment: A Problem of Industry*, 1909

Just as Rowntree established that poverty was not the fault of its victims, so Beveridge — then a young civil servant at Winston Churchill's Board of Trade — made it clear that unemployment was beyond the control of the unemployed. The book established the idea of state control of industry to prevent the waste of valuable manpower, and saw insurance as a way of protecting the individual.

In the year that Beveridge's book was published, the Labour Exchanges Act was passed. It set up a network of exchanges run by the state which are still with us under the name of Job Centres. Along with Acts to create half-day closing for shops and minimum wages and maximum hours in some other trades, this was another move away from *laissez-faire*.

However, it was the National Health Insurance Act (1911) which was the major reform of the pre-war years. Part II of the Act created unemployment insurance for some two million men, in seven key trades where loss of work through trade slump was most common, such as shipbuilding and engineering. Workers contributed 2d. a week, the employer 1d. and the government 1d. For this, workers would receive benefit of just over 6s. a week for up to 15 weeks of unemployment. Although it was far from a living wage, and left the

The National Insurance Act explained. Although it was passed in 1911, it came into force two years later

unemployed to the mercy of the Poor Law Guardians or various charities when the 15 weeks expired, it was at least a start. It was only meant to provide short-term assistance, in conjunction with the labour exchanges, for those between jobs — not a long-term income for those who could find no work.

Part I of the Act, which provided insurance against sickness, caused great uproar among Conservatives and in the House of Lords. Many peers were still outraged by Lloyd George's 'People's Budget' of 1909, which had begun the practice of taxing the wealthy to obtain money for public spending. Yet only a small proportion of the cost of the new scheme came from taxes. Every man earning under £160 a year had to pay 4d. a week, to which the government added 2d. and the employer 3d., to give the worker 'ninepence for fourpence'. In return, when ill, he received 10s. a week for 26 weeks, and free treatment from a doctor. The scheme did not cover hospital treatment except for consumption, in what Lloyd George called the 'sanatorium benefit'. Working women paid 3d., and were entitled to between 9s. and 12s. a week in sickness benefit. There was also a maternity benefit, and sanatorium benefit as for men. Married women were not covered unless they worked, and there were no benefits for the worker's dependants.

It was not only the Conservatives who were against the Bill. Friendly societies thought that they would be put out of business, and doctors feared they would lose their independence, causing standards of medicine to fall. Against the background of a crisis caused by the House of Lords' refusal to pass his 1909 budget, Lloyd George negotiated with both groups. The friendly societies were renamed 'approved societies' and were asked to administer the scheme, and the doctors were to be paid 6s. for each member of their 'panel' of working patients. At last, in 1911, the Bill became law.

Lloyd George defended the Bill passionately:

> *Our object, our goal ought to be enough to maintain efficiency for
> every man, woman and child. The individual demands it, the State
> needs it, humanity cries for it, religion insists upon it. But for
> millions of the poor a bare subsistence is difficult to win and easy to
> lose. The illness of the wage earner in hundreds of thousands
> of households, trade depression, a change of fashions precipitates
> thousands into destitution, poverty and privation. . . . All their money
> is spent on food, shelter, raiment, and nothing can be spared for the
> storeroom when the needs of illness and unemployment come.*

raiment: clothing

David Lloyd George: speech at Birmingham, 10 June 1911

By the end of 1911, Britain had compulsory insurance of the lowest-
paid workers against unemployment and sickness; a state network of
labour exchanges; and non-contributory old age pensions. But it still
had the old Poor Law, unrevised despite the advice of the Royal
Commission's two reports; and there was no provision for treatment
of the poor in hospital, or for dental or eye care. The Housing and
Town Planning Act of 1909 had given local authorities the power to
control building in the suburbs; but slums remained in many cities
and rural areas. The number of organisations involved in helping
those in need had not decreased since 1900. Had Britain really
advanced towards a welfare state?

Both Winston Churchill, at the Board of Trade, and Lloyd George,
the Chancellor of the Exchequer, saw the scheme as only a beginning.
Another passage from the Chancellor's Birmingham speech suggests
that it would have developed further if the war had not intervened:

> *I never said this Bill was a final solution. I am not putting it
> forward as a complete remedy. It is one of a series. We are advancing
> on the road, but it is an essential part of the journey.*

Questions

1 What was the original purpose of unemployment benefit?

2 In what ways do you think the researches of Beveridge and
   Rowntree influenced Lloyd George when he was forming his
   national insurance policy? Give your answers in chart form,
   noting the source (Rowntree or Beveridge); the point it makes;
   and the corresponding point made by Lloyd George.

3 It is 1911 and you are the wife of a 43-year-old shipyard
   labourer. Your rent is 3s. 6d. a week, and food for your family
   takes up almost all of the remainder of your husband's 14s.
   weekly wage. Write a paragraph about how you manage on
   10s. 6d. a week. Use the budget on page 13 to gain an idea
   of prices. Finish by saying what you think of the new
   insurance scheme.

WAR, BOOM AND DEPRESSION

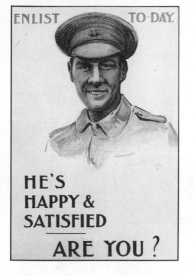

HE'S
HAPPY &
SATISFIED

ARE YOU ?

A Parliamentary Recruiting Committee poster, 1914

When the farmer stopped my pay because it was raining and we couldn't thrash, I said to my seventeen-year-old mate, 'B----- him. We'll go off and join the army.' It was 14th March 1914.... In my four months' training with the regiment I put on nearly a stone in weight and got a bit taller. They said it was the food, but it was really because for the first time in my life there had been no strenuous work. I want to say this simply as a fact, that village people in Suffolk in my day were worked to death. It literally happened. We were all damned glad to have got off the farms. I had 7s. a week and sent my mother half of it. If you did this, the government would add another 3s. 6d. — so my mother got 7s.

Leonard Thompson, quoted in Ronald Blythe's book,
Akenfield, 1969

Questions

1   What does this passage reveal about the health of farm workers at this time? Give reasons for your answer.

2   Why did Leonard Thompson join the army? Is the poster intended to appeal to people with similar feelings? Explain your answer clearly.

Leonard Thompson joined the army during the last months of peace. In August 1914, when World War I began, many thousands of men volunteered. For the great majority, the main reason was a sense of duty to the nation. At the same time, there was the knowledge that their dependants would be paid an allowance by the government, while they themselves would be fed and clothed by the army. Very few could have foreseen the horrors of trench warfare, and for the first 18 months recruiting went well.

In 1916, however, the need for soldiers was so great that the government introduced conscription — compulsory service in the forces. Young single men were called up first, then those belonging to older age groups. Before being accepted, they were given a medical inspection, and a report on the results of such examinations was published in 1918:

Of every nine men of military age in Great Britain, on the average three were perfectly fit and healthy; two were upon a definitely infirm plane of health and strength, whether from some disability or some failure in development; three were incapable of undergoing more

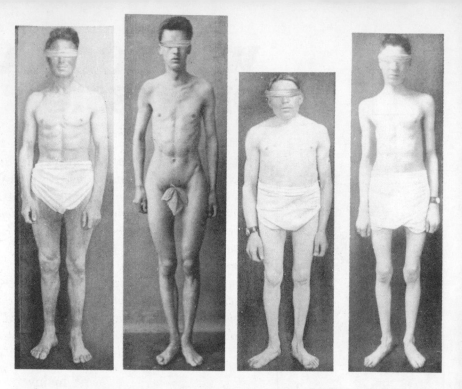

Grades of men (left to right, 1–4) examined for the army, from the 1918 report. The government expected 70 per cent to be in Grade I, but only 36 per cent were fit enough, while 41 per cent were in the lowest two grades

than a very moderate degree of physical exertion and could almost (in view of their age) be described with justice as physical wrecks; and the remaining man as a chronic invalid with a precarious hold upon life.

Report upon the Physical Examination of Men of Military Age by National Service Medical Boards from November 1st 1917–October 31st 1918, 1918

The report went on to list the men's ailments and urged a study of their causes:

This information, once harvested, should indicate unmistakeably the direction in which efforts should be made to improve the national health by preventing what is preventable, and by ameliorating or palliating what is unavoidable.

ameliorating: making better
palliating: making it easier to endure

Questions

1   Judging from the information given in Chapter 1, say why four out of every nine conscripts were 'physical wrecks'.

2   Look closely at the second extract from the 1918 report, which suggests that something should be done about 'the national health'. What attitude towards people does this suggest?

3   The report's findings and recommendations were an important factor in the growth of the welfare state. Why was this? Try to give several reasons.

A munitions factory canteen

It was not only servicemen who were involved in the war of 1914–18. Unlike earlier wars, it began to involve those at home, especially women. They drove lorries, made shells and took over businesses run by men who were away fighting. The greatest need was to increase output of armaments and, to do this, nearly a million women were working in munitions factories by 1918. Many had to move to new areas, staying with local families or in specially built towns. Nurseries were provided for the children of women workers, and canteens and other welfare facilities were built. Much attention was given to feeding workers properly, as a contemporary document explains:

> *There is now an overwhelming body of experience which proves that productive output in regard to quality, amount and speed is largely dependent upon the physical efficiency of the worker.*
> *Ministry of Munitions' Health of Munition Workers Committee,*
> *Memorandum No 2: Industrial Canteens, 1915*

The government did all it could to encourage firms to build canteens; it exempted their cost from excess profits tax and published details and plans of suitable buildings. This was state action in the area of people's wellbeing taken to a degree unheard of in peacetime, and it did much to improve workers' health.

Yet despite this, after 1917 there were often food shortages because of submarine attacks on ships bringing supplies to Britain. Military authorities began to report that the morale of the troops in France was being weakened by references to shortages of food in letters from home. At the same time, too, there was a feeling in government circles that the poor should not be made to suffer more than the wealthy because of food shortages.

These forces all combined to bring about the introduction of price controls and food rationing schemes, under which every person was allowed only a fixed amount of basic provisions. Local schemes in London and Birmingham led the way in 1917, and a national scheme run by the Ministry of Food followed in 1918. This resulted in a deluge of government orders; the catalogue of government publications for the last year of the war has ten and a half pages listing titles of ration orders covering meat, margarine, milk, oils and many other foods. Coal, too, came under control, to try to ensure warmth and cooking facilities for all. Leaflets on nutrition and balanced diets were circulated nationally; experts were employed to demonstrate how to cook cheap, wholesome dishes; and 'communal feeding centres' were set up.

At the same time another factor had unexpectedly begun to help improve the nation's health: people were getting better wages. In addition, many of the poorest people – especially women – were going out to work for the first time, earning a reasonable living wage. The combined effect of better incomes, equal provisions for all and the spread of knowledge about nutrition was remarkable. Infant mortality – the death rate of very young babies – fell in almost every area, and people's general standard of health rose. A modern historian sums up:

We are thus left with the paradox...that, because of armed conflict, the country came to be a healthier place to live in.
Jay Winter: 'Army and Society: the Demographic Context', Ian Beckett and Keith Simpson (eds), *A Nation in Arms*, 1985

Questions

1   Give three reasons why the government took action to improve nutrition during World War I.

2   What is the 'paradox' referred to in the extract above? Does it suggest anything to you about the government's attitude to war and the wellbeing of the people?

The Ministry of Food was only one of the new bodies created during the war which, taken together, added up to an increase of state control undreamt of in earlier years. The old spirit of *laissez-faire* seemed to have disappeared as a result of the fighting. The Ministry of Pensions was created to handle the claims of wounded and disabled servicemen and their dependants. Towards the end of the war plans were laid to bring together public health, medicine and health insurance under a single Ministry of Health, which was founded in 1919. For the first time in Britain it was accepted that the state had a responsibility for the welfare of its citizens, in return for the contribution they made to national output.

The new mechanism for social welfare was introduced at a time when there was a growing desire for change. Everyone had made sacrifices in the war; few families were untouched by injury or bereavement. In 1917 a Ministry of Reconstruction had been set up with the aim, in Lloyd George's words, of 'moulding a better world'. The feeling that the years of sacrifice must be made worthwhile was well expressed by a young officer who was appalled at the conditions in which a young widow, whose husband had been killed in France, had to live with her small children:

> *Is this one of the things for which we have fought? Has all the suffering and sacrifice been endured for the sake of things as they are? It is not enough that we have fought for the present, for a condition of things in which slums can exist.... Oh! England, awake, rise up in the greatness of your coming victory and say 'there shall be no more slums'.*
>
> 'An Amateur Officer': *After Victory*, 1917

'Homes fit for heroes...'

In the last months of the war, a report appeared which set new standards for the houses of working people. Every house should have an indoor bathroom and lavatory; rows of houses should be at least 21 metres apart and there should be no more than 12 houses to the acre (nineteenth-century back-to-back houses were often two or three times that density); they should have gardens, not back yards; and they should be built of varied materials to avoid 'the deadly monotony ...which is associated with so many housing schemes'. Perhaps the most important provision was this:

> *We regard it as essential that each house should contain as a minimum three rooms on the ground floor (living-room, parlour and scullery) and three bedrooms above — two of these being capable of containing two beds. A larder and a bathroom are essential.*
>
> The Tudor Walters Report, Command Paper 9191, 1918

Plans for working-class houses, from the Tudor Walters Report, 1918

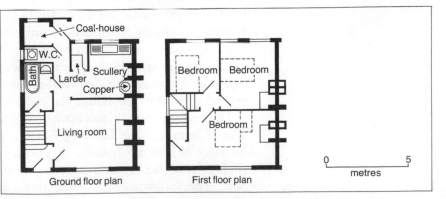

21

This was a striking new departure in the design of low-cost housing for working people. So, too, was the report's suggestion of designing whole areas of housing, roads, schools and shops. Both ideas had previously only been carried out in expensive private schemes such as Letchworth Garden City. But the Tudor Walters Report was only the first stage: action to clear slums and build the 'homes fit for heroes' which Lloyd George promised could come only from an Act of Parliament.

Question

Compare the houses described and illustrated in the Tudor Walters Report with the one shown on page 6. Then copy out and complete the following table, to show the difference in the facilities they offer:

Victorian house	Tudor Walters house	Result of difference
No bathroom	Indoor bathroom	Improved cleanliness and health
Cooking done in living room	Separate area for cooking	Coal fumes and cooking smells kept from living area

---

At first, it seemed as if the report would be put into practice. Under the Housing and Town Planning Act of 1919, local authorities had to clear slums, with the aid of government grants. Rehousing proceeded quickly; the number of houses built in 1922 soared to 110 000 — more than in any year until the 1950s. But this did not last.

After World War I there was a boom in trade, because people were anxious to buy the goods that had been unobtainable during the war. Soon, however, the demand was satisfied and the economy collapsed. The government was forced to cut spending, and education and housing were badly affected. In 1921 the housing programme was stopped; building continued on only those houses which had already been started. It was the first instance of the problem which was to hinder public spending on every aspect of social welfare throughout the years between the two world wars: the need to cut spending in response to acute economic depression.

Despite this, much was achieved. Things began to pick up in 1923 when Chamberlain's Housing Act was passed. This gave subsidies to builders of private houses, to encourage better-off workers to buy their own homes, thereby making more rented accommodation available. The following year, Wheatley's Housing Act gave subsidies to builders of rented housing. These Acts, together with the boom in private house building of the twenties, which sent ribbons of semi-detached houses trailing through the fields outside many cities, greatly improved living conditions for many people, as a direct result of government action.

Yet these developments did little to help the very poor. For this reason, the Housing Act of 1930 forced local authorities to draw up five-year plans of slum clearance and paid them a subsidy for each family that was rehoused. As a result many of the worst slums were cleared in some cities. A joiner from St Helens recalls:

> *I've seen bugs in houses, when we worked in demolition.... I think it was the conditions of damp and abject poverty, with plaster infested, and the lack of personal attention – not realizing that these bugs wanted attacking. You had to get special candles and spray everything with formalin.... When we went into the houses we were debugging, we had elastic bands round our trousers to [keep out] the flecks, as they were called.... There were rats running up and down the place and in all the houses in Napier Street, New Cross Street and Talbot Street....*
>
> Quoted in C. Forman's book, *Industrial Town*, 1978

In the cities, many local authorities built flats instead of houses of the sort Tudor Walters recommended. Some, such as the recently demolished Quarry Hill development in Leeds, were disasters, forcing people to live in vast, anonymous buildings which lacked the close contact and friendship that had existed in even the worst slums.

Slum clearance in action: Kennington Road, London

Others, such as the London flats described below, were more successful and attractive:

> The layout . . . is admirable, and to my mind meets some of the most pressing necessities of working-class housing. The living-rooms are spacious, and the kitchen and scullery, with gas cooker, sink and draining-board, have all those gadgets which are the housewife's joy. A continual supply of hot water night and day helps the washing, and a compact bathroom, with hand-basin, is an unmitigated boon.
>
> The lowest rent for two rooms is 7s. 6d. a week, up to 10s. for three and 14s. for five — living-room, scullery, etc., and three bedrooms.
>
> Mrs Cecil Chesterton: *I Lived in a Slum*, 1936

unmitigated boon: vast improvement

Question

Draw up a table like the one on page 22. Using the drawing and Mrs Chesterton's description, complete the table to show the difference between a 1930s flat and a Victorian terraced house.

Between the two world wars, housing had its successes and its failures. In some areas, slums were cleared and replaced by new estates of high-quality houses which still offer good accommodation today. For those with new houses, it was a good time. As a modern architectural historian has pointed out:

> Never again were we to build so extensively and indiscriminately, nor were we ever to satisfy so many people so quickly.
>
> Anthony Quiney: *House and Home*, 1986

Elsewhere, slums remained. The clearing subsidies were removed in 1933, but in 1935 another Housing Act made overcrowding an offence for local authorities. Even the target of demolishing a quarter of a million houses and giving a million people well-built, clean homes had not been met by 1939. However, the city slums were soon to be demolished — not by local authority workmen but by Hitler's bombs.

Health and pensions between the wars

Although sickness benefit was raised to 18s. a week in 1918, the years that followed brought no real changes in the system of health care. Like housing, it suffered from the need to save money: in 1926 the state's contribution was cut, and in 1932 the benefit for working married women fell too.

Treatment from doctors was still as it had been under the 1911 Act, with most patients having to pay for consultations and Poor

Law doctors for those classed as paupers. A doctor in the north of England recalls:

> *Only the men were on the National Health that Lloyd George brought in. They had to pay for their families, and that was the collection system. The better-class people had accounts. If someone never paid, you could put him in the petty debt court. The commonest way was to cross him off your list.*
>
> *But we're painting a very gloomy picture. There was another side to it: the medical work, and the decency and humanity that you found as you went round your patients. They were good and honest people. Those who couldn't pay . . . [well,] you cut your coat according to your cloth. If a patient contributed a small sum a week, even if the book figure was ten times that, you kept visiting. If they died, they died. You scored your pen through it.*
>
> Quoted in C. Forman's book, *Industrial Town*, 1978

One of the biggest problems was that sickness benefit did not include allowances for the wife and children of a working man whereas, from 1921, unemployment benefit did. If a man became ill, the family income would drop seriously as a result, whether he was in work or unemployed. Everyone knew that this was ridiculous, but there were two great obstacles which prevented the joining up of the two systems. One was pressure from the friendly societies − the private insurance firms who ran the scheme of health payments for the government. No government wanted to offend such powerful financial bodies by taking a major source of income away from them. The other was the series of financial crises in the twenties and thirties which prevented any far-reaching reforms because of the need to save money.

Health care at a local level: subsidised school milk, Lambeth, 1929

Some progress was, however, made. The 1929 Local Government Act finally replaced the Poor Law Guardians with Public Assistance Committees. The same Act allowed local authorities to take over Poor Law infirmaries as municipal hospitals, and the decade saw the formation of many such institutions and the introduction of specialised clinics. There were improvements, too, in health care for school-children, with subsidised milk for all and holiday schemes for poor children living in cities. The 1918 Maternity and Child Welfare Act empowered local authorities to provide antenatal and children's clinics, and in 1936 the Midwives Act made it compulsory for local authorities to appoint midwives. Together the two Acts considerably improved women's health. Yet despite all these advances there were still major gaps in medical services, most especially in hospital provision — as the demands of the war years were to make clear.

Meanwhile, in 1925, a contributory old age pension had been introduced for manual workers. It was paid for by contributions from the worker, the employer and the state, and gave pensions to retired people between the ages of 65 and 70. At 70, they changed to the non-contributory scheme begun in 1909. In 1929 the scheme was extended to include widows over 60, and in 1937 it was extended again to cover most office and clerical workers.

There was, then, slow growth rather than rapid change in health care and pensions between the wars, but throughout these years another problem dominated social policy: unemployment.

Questions

1 What attitude towards the patients is shown in the doctor's recollections on page 25? Use quotations from the passage to support your answer.

2 What do you think was the effect of charging patients for treatment and visits from the doctor? In your answer refer to the patients' health and their attitude to the doctor.

Unemployment

When the thousands of men and women in the armed forces finally returned to civilian life after the long and weary years of fighting, there was a mood of hope and confidence. Now that the suffering was ended, they could set to work to build a brighter future. Members of the forces were given non-contributory payments to tide them over until they found work, although in the postwar boom there were few employment problems. In 1920 the number of workers covered by unemployment insurance was increased to some 12 million, including almost everyone earning less than £5 a week. Experts

calculated that this would produce a fund for unemployment benefit for four per cent of the population. No one dreamed that, in the thirties, the rate would be four times that figure.

The hope was short-lived. By June 1921, two million people were out of work as the postwar boom collapsed. The fund from unemployment insurance contributions could not hope to cover benefits, and the rate was cut from 20s. to 15s. a week. For the first time, money was taken from the Exchequer – government income from taxes and investments – to supplement the fund. In an effort to cut payments, the government introduced a 'test' – to receive benefit people had to prove that they were 'seeking work'. If they could not, they received no payment. For these people, as well as those who had made no contributions for unemployment insurance, and those who had exhausted their benefit, there was only the Poor Law, with all the disgrace that 'relief' involved. Applying for such help was often humiliating:

We had to go early in the morning for this relief, because there were hundreds in the queue outside the chapel where they gave out the relief-slips. I wonder would it cost them very much effort to be only

27

decently civil to the ones who apply for relief? Or do they purposely pick men who have no sympathy or patience? I did not hear the officers speak one decent word during that period when we had to go there weekly — they seemed to hate the applicants.

B.L. Coombes: *These Poor Hands*, 1939

Not all relief officers were so unsympathetic:

A lot of the houses were beautifully kept. The people were proud of their cottage property. None of my brother officers would urge them to sell anything. I used to say, 'Keep your little home together,' and they did.

Quoted in C. Forman's book, *Industrial Town*, 1978

Questions

1 In the Coombes passage, what was the relief officers' attitude to the applicants? Quote words and phrases to support your answer.

2 In what way did the attitude of the relief officers in the second passage differ?

3 Both of these passages were written some time after the events they describe, and both writers see things in a very personal way. How do these points affect the value of the passages for the historian?

4 Coombes was a miner in South Wales; the writer of the other passage worked in the industrial north-west of England. What do these facts, and the difference in attitudes shown in the passages, suggest about how relief was administered in Britain at this time?

Although limitations were placed on unemployment benefit in 1921, some improvements were also made. A system of 'uncovenanted benefit' — payment not covered by the worker's contributions — was introduced and, in November, payments were made for dependent wives and children.

The Unemployment Insurance Act of 1927 tried to return to the idea of insurance, rather than payment from the government, for unemployed people. A worker would receive 'standard benefit' if he or she had made 30 contributions over a period of two years. People who had made fewer or no contributions could claim 'transitional benefit' for a limited time. This meant that they would not suffer the disgrace of Poor Law relief which had so angered B.L. Coombes.

Yet these advances were soon threatened by the growing financial crisis which followed the Wall Street Crash and the international trade depression. Ramsay MacDonald's Labour Government was

The following table shows the proposed weekly rates for the several classes of insured persons now entitled to benefit, together with the present weekly rate.

	Present Rates.		Proposed Rates.	
	s.	d.	s.	d.
Man	17	0 ...	15	3
Woman	15	0 ...	13	6
Adult dependant ...	9	0 ...	8	0
Child dependant ...	2	0 ...	2	0
Young man	14	0 ...	12	6
Young woman	12	0 ...	10	9
Juveniles—				
Boys aged 17	9	0 ...	8	0
Girls aged 17	7	6 ...	6	9
Boys aged 16	6	0 ...	5	6
Girls aged 16	5	0 ...	4	6

The saving estimated to result from this reduction is £12,800,000.

The full savings for 1932 are as follows:

	£
Reductions of emoluments of Ministers, Members of Parliament, Judges, Civil Servants, and members of the Defence Services	4,534,000
Defence Services (in addition to reductions of £3,614,000 in pay and pensions)	5,000,000
Education (Great Britain) ...	10,300,000
University Grants	150,000
Ministry of Health and Scottish Department of Health...	1,250,000
Police (Great Britain)	500,000
Agriculture (Great Britain)...	655,000
Forestry	478,000
Empire Marketing Board	250,000
Colonial Development Fund...	250,000
Unemployment Grants	500,000
Unemployment Insurance— (a) Reduction of expenditure from the Unemployment Fund	25,800,000
(b) Increased income of the Unemployment Fund from contributions of employers and workmen	10,000,000
Road Fund	7,865,000
Miscellaneous	2,500,000
Total	70,032,000

The 1931 budget explained: tables from The Morning Post, *11 September 1931*

The sign of the pawnshop, which dominated many lives in the thirties

accused of adding to the cost of benefit by removing the 'seeking work' test in 1930, and by paying the 'transitional benefits' directly from the Exchequer. Its critics said that this was increasing spending at a time when everything should be done to cut costs. Transitional benefit was certainly expensive: it cost £19 million in its first year. Bankers told the government that the only way to stop the crisis was to cut spending; yet for a Labour government, committed to improving conditions for working people, the idea of cutting unemployment benefit was hard to accept. MacDonald reluctantly agreed that cuts had to be made but, as his Cabinet was divided, he resigned. In the face of the crisis he was asked to form a national government – a coalition with the Conservatives. In September the Chancellor of the Exchequer, Philip Snowden, was forced to make savage cuts in an emergency budget. The budget White Paper contained this paragraph:

There is to be a reduction of the weekly benefit rates in respect of Unemployment Insurance of 10 per cent, rounded off to the nearest threepence. This reduction does not apply to the allowances for dependent children. A needs test is to be instituted for persons drawing transitional benefits.

Transitional benefit was to be administered by the Public Assistance Committees. They had the power to investigate the income and resources of people claiming benefit. This investigation – the hated 'means test' – involved finding out the income and evaluating the possessions of every member of the family and refusing to give any help until the last item had been sold. It was a humiliating experience and, when Snowden's budget speech had long been forgotten, the means test would still be mentioned with anguish in many homes.

Questions

1 Give two reasons why unemployment benefit was cut in the 1931 budget.

2 Philip Snowden claimed that the 'burden of sacrifice' was to be borne by everyone equally. Was this a true claim? Support your answer with reasons.

Memoirs of the unemployed

In the early thirties, the BBC published in *The Listener* a series of short pieces by unemployed workers. Later collected and published in a book called *Memoirs of the Unemployed* (H.L. Beales and R.S. Lambert, eds. 1934) they offer a range of views of what life was like 'on the dole':

Alfred Smith gives his wife his £2 7s. 6d. benefit. Their weekly budget is:

	s.	d.
Rent	14	6
Clothes club	6	0
Insurance	1	8
Coal club	3	0
Coke	1	0
Lighting and fittings	3	0
Bread	6	0
Other food	16	0
	2 11	2

'The Smiths say they can only live by getting into debt', Picture Post, 21 January 1939

Bailiffs evict a mother and her eight children from their flat in Bermondsey, 1932

My unemployment benefit came to an end in March 1932, when I was disallowed because I had not qualified for the necessary contributory period of thirty weeks. After this I was given a food ticket for 23s. a week, which continued until January, 1933, when it was stopped because of the Means Test. Before the stoppage our income was over the minimum limit of £2 17s. 6d. So now we have to depend on the boys, and they have to keep all six of us, including my wife and the two children who are still going to school.

A South Wales miner

Not only manual workers suffered. An advertising designer earning £1000 a year — worth about £25 000 today — had not contributed to the insurance scheme. This is what happened when he lost his job:

I was ineligible for unemployment pay, and was forced to apply to the Public Assistance Committee. They refused to help us, and the sale of oddments began.... My difficulty was to get sufficient money for food, and to pay the rent was out of the question. Eventually the bailiffs were put in. They were very decent and left the beds and bedding and a few kitchen things.

An unemployed businessman

Women workers also suffered:

I do not know on Fridays who to pay first. I get the food from the nearest shop on 'strap' and I must pay that debt or there's no more forthcoming for the rest of the week. The rent is 5s. 6d. a week, and I must not get far behind with that. It's the children's clothes that worry me most. They want so much feeding and they are always wanting their shoes soled. I cannot let them go without shoes in the bad weather, but that means that they must go without food.

A married factory worker

For the young, things were no different:

> *I hunt for work everywhere, I answer adverts., write and enquire on different firms, call personally, but it's all hopeless. The only jobs I get are temporary and I'm fed up with life. I feel I'd like to smash a shop window, just to hear the glass rattle, and the only thing that stops me is I've seen other poor devils who are lots worse off than myself, and I'm thankful I'm not in the same boat. I am just turned twenty-one years of age and have spent the last three 'New Years' unemployed.*

The carpenter's younger son

Unemployment often affected the family's health:

> *My wife is often very poorly without being really ill. She has long fits of depression and then gets asthma and bronchitis. When she has had a bad bout for a month or two she seems to shake it off and go on all right for a few weeks. Her worst troubles are her eyes and teeth. She cannot see to thread a needle or read, and often complains that her eyes hurt her, but we cannot afford glasses which are at least 15s. Her teeth cause abscesses but we cannot afford to go to the dentist at 4s. 6d. a visit.*

A skilled millwright

Workers from Jarrow, marching to London to protest about unemployment in 1936, receive food from workers as they pass through a town

1 Apart from shortage of money, unemployment had many other adverse effects on people's lives. List all those that are mentioned in the passages on pages 30–31.

2 You are a 35-year-old skilled factory worker thrown out of your job by the depression. Using the *Memoirs* and the illustrations in this section, write an account of how you spend an average day, describing your feelings and hopes.

By 1934 the economy had improved so much that the 1931 cuts in benefit could be restored and the insurance scheme extended to cover fourteen and a half million workers. The National Insurance Act of that year was important for making clear the difference between insurance and benefit for unemployment.

Part I of the Act concerned insurance, and laid down that benefit would be paid from the fund of money collected by contributions for a maximum of 26 weeks. It would be paid by an independent committee, to keep it separate from political pressures.

Part II of the Act set up an Unemployment Assistance Board, a national body which took over the role of the Public Assistance Committees, helping those with no income or right to other benefits. In making the division between unemployment benefit and social security payments, the Act set up a system which still survives. Although the UAB actually paid less than the old Committees in some areas, it was generally seen to be an improvement on the earlier system.

Throughout the thirties, governments and local authorities had tried to do what they could for those who were out of work. What they achieved varied considerably over the years and in different areas, yet there is no doubt that many people suffered severe hardship throughout the decade. It was only in the very late thirties, when Britain began to re-arm in the face of Hitler's Germany, that employment began to rise once more. And by then, as one writer made clear at the time, the cost in money and human suffering had been great:

The theory during the whole grim period has been that the cheapest (and therefore, of course, the best) method is to give the men just enough to exist themselves and keep their families alive, not even in good health, but just alive. The result is colossal waste . . . waste of men, waste of intelligence, waste of physical strength, waste of invaluable national assets . . . . England is beginning to discover her shortage now that she wants skilled men at her armament trades and strong men for her defence.

Ellen Wilkinson: *The Town that was Murdered*, 1939

Alfred Smith tells the clerk: 'No work'. He has had no regular work for three years and he comes to the Labour Exchange three times a week. He signs on, gets two tickets signed, draws his unemployment benefit. Before he leaves the Exchange, he carefully studies the list of vacant posts in the hall. Will there be a chance for him to-day? Will his luck change? Picture Post, *21 January 1939*

Questions

1 How would you describe the tone of the extract on page 32? Is it, for example, angry, serious or cynical? Why do you think the writer says that the cheapest method is 'of course' the best?

2 What attitude towards those in government, and their treatment of the unemployment crisis, is suggested by this tone?

3 Ellen Wilkinson was the Labour MP for Jarrow, a town in which two-thirds of the workers were unemployed throughout the thirties. How does this information affect the value of the passage for the historian?

WAR AND SOCIAL CHANGE

Thursday, 31 August 1939: Walthamstow, east London. From the district's schools, several columns of children emerge, each led by a teacher. The children walk in pairs, some smiling and laughing, others quietly weeping. A few have kitbags or suitcases; many have shopping baskets or pillowcases. All carry small cardboard boxes and have labels attached to their clothes. In the boxes are gas masks; on the labels is written each child's name and address. The columns move along the streets of Victorian terraced houses, teachers holding up the traffic while the children turn and cross to the other side. At Blackhorse Road railway station they crowd into waiting trains which pull swiftly away into the Essex countryside.

What was happening in Walthamstow was also happening in Leeds, Sheffield, Birmingham and every large city: the removal of children from areas at greatest risk from bombing. The children were 'the evacuees' or, more simply, 'the vacs'. As long ago as 1931 a committee had been set up to arrange the evacuation of cities in case of war. Now, with war a matter of days away, the plan had been put into practice by the Ministry of Health. Between this Thursday and Sunday 3 September, when war was declared against Hitler's Germany, one and a half million children, expectant mothers and sick or disabled people were moved to the safety of country areas.

Children walking to Blackhorse Road station for the evacuation train

There, they were billeted with local people who received a government allowance of 10s. 6d. for the first child and 8s. for any others, with lower allowances for the children's mothers if they accompanied them.

The plan was another stage in the state's increasing involvement in the care of the individual. Moving such large numbers of people was a major feat — 4000 special trains were needed in London alone. What happened when they reached their destination, however, was often less successful. The experience of 17 000 children, mothers and teachers, evacuated by boat from Dagenham, on the eastern outskirts of London, was typical:

On the arrival of the boats the reception authorities were aghast at the numbers. No organisation existed for dealing with them. Schools and other buildings were opened, but bedding and blankets did not exist. In some cases for four days they lived — teachers, mothers and children — on an official diet of milk, apples and cheese, sleeping on straw covered by grain bags. There was no lack of human effort on the part of the townspeople — the problem was beyond adequate handling.

Richard Padley and Margaret Cole (eds):
Evacuation Survey: A Report to the Fabian Society, 1940

Questions

1   According to the report, was the evacuation well organised? Give reasons for your answer.

2   Who, according to the report, was responsible for the conditions met by the evacuees at their destination?

As well as the accommodation problems that they experienced when they first arrived in the country, the evacuees faced difficulties in finding people to take them in for a longer period. Instead of allocating children to particular local people, the authorities simply asked for volunteers who would choose which children they wanted to take. Children 'paraded around while householders took their pick', according to one eyewitness. The healthy, clean and attractive went first; the sickly and underfed stayed, often tearfully, until last. In terms of organisation, the scheme was clearly not a complete success: the state still had much to learn about organising people, and experience gained at this time was to be put to use much later, when the Ministry of Health had to deal with large numbers of people at the start of the National Health Service.

In terms of the growth of the welfare state, however, the most important feature of evacuation was that, for the first time, the real state of people living in the crowded cities was realised by those who

Evacuation was a partnership between the state and the individual in the manner of the later welfare state, as this Ministry of Health poster makes clear

It might be YOU!

CARING FOR EVACUEES IS A NATIONAL SERVICE

ISSUED BY THE MINISTRY OF HEALTH

lived in the more prosperous country areas. Most of the children who were evacuated came from poor homes — parents who could afford to do so made their own arrangements — and their new hosts were appalled by what they saw. Horror stories spread quickly through the shires: the 'vacs' had fleas and nits, never took baths, and knew nothing about basic personal hygiene. Some of the stories were true:

> *Evacuees came from the toughest of a tough city and their notions of hygiene were distinctly primitive. They came from Liverpool. About 20% of the children and at least 45% of the women were lousy.*
>
> Tom Harrisson and Charles Madge:
> *War Begins at Home*, 1940

Gradually, collections were made for new clothes for the children, and they learned to accept the standards of cleanliness of their foster parents. Many fled back to the cities in the early days of war, but many more stayed, to discover a wholly new world away from the squalor of the slums. For both evacuees and their hosts, it was an eye-opening experience. The idea that, after the war, such conditions must be wiped out, began to gain acceptance: it was another step towards the welfare state. A contemporary account by a Norfolk doctor expresses this well:

What the ultimate result of the evacuation scheme will be it is too early to surmise. It has, however, brought into clear relief certain evils of our social system which call for action. Five months of intimate experience of the evacuated children have demonstrated the fact that the poorer the home and the more densely populated the area from which the children come, the longer have they taken to respond to good air and decent house room. The agricultural labourer has low wages, and his cottage is often poor and old-fashioned. Nevertheless it was a surprise and shock to the country people to find that there could be such poverty, that there could be such appalling housing conditions as prevailed in the homes of many of their foster-children.

Richard Padley and Margaret Cole (eds):
Evacuation Survey: A Report to the Fabian Society, 1940

Questions

1   You are a 12-year-old evacuee from Dagenham. At the end of your first day in the country, write a postcard to your parents at home.

2   You are a woman aged 50 married to a country doctor. Write a diary entry for Saturday, 2 September 1939, describing how you spent the day looking after evacuee children and their mothers at a church hall, while they waited to be given homes with local people.

Rationing and health

Writing in 1940, a country doctor judged that evacuated children 'appear taller and heavier, and are brighter and more healthy in appearance' than when they first arrived. Evacuees certainly enjoyed a better diet during their stay in the country, and this was only one aspect of a concern with food and nutrition which, in one form or another, affected everyone during the war years. In World War I rationing had been introduced at a late stage in the fighting. This time it was introduced almost as soon as war was declared; the first rationing schemes came into effect in January 1940. Everyone had to register with a food shop and could buy only limited amounts of basic foods each week in exchange for 'coupons' cut from ration books. Some foods – bread and potatoes, for example – were not rationed at first, but others were available only in very small amounts.

Foods which were imported were particularly scarce, and the meat and sugar rations for adults were reduced sharply as the war continued. To supplement the rations, as much food as possible was produced at home. Waste ground was ploughed up and sown with grain; local

MEALS *without* MEAT

Seven appetising meals without using the meat ration

ALL RECIPES FOR 4 PERSONS   ALL SPOONS LEVEL

FOODS TO USE INSTEAD OF MEAT

Meat is a body-building food and can be replaced only by one of the other body-building foods.

1. The best are : Milk (fresh, household or canned), Cheese, Fish (fresh or canned) and Eggs (fresh or dried).
2. Second best are : Soya flour, Dried Peas, Beans and Lentils, Oatmeal and Semolina.

Our bodies use a mixture of the two kinds very well.

No. 29

councils took over land for use as allotments; and neighbours banded together to form 'pig clubs' – each club kept a pig which consumed scraps and provided a little bacon. The Ministry of Food carried out a campaign to tell people how to use less-familiar foods. Its 'Food Facts' appeared regularly in the newspapers; 30-second 'Food Flashes' were screened in cinemas; and leaflets on meals without meat, using cheese and making jam from hedgerow fruits were printed and distributed by the thousand.

Strange new foods appeared to take the place of scarce items:

We never starved, but we ate some...funny things. Best was American dried egg. You poured a thin trickle into the frying-pan, then as it cooked it blew up like a balloon, till it was two inches thick, like a big yellow hump-backed whale.

Tyneside boy, quoted in Robert Westall's book, *Children of the Blitz*, 1985

Left: *a leaflet encouraging people to eat meatless meals*

Right: *'Food Facts' appeared throughout the war in newspapers. State involvement with people's diets has never been greater*

FOOD FACTS

Children's choice

You won't need to worry about Winter if you will just remember to give the children a serving of *lightly cooked* green vegetable every day, plenty of *jacket potatoes*, and a good helping of *raw shredded vegetables* in a salad or a sandwich. These with the full rations and allowances, with porridge and bread to fill up the corners, will keep the children fighting fit throughout the coldest weather.

MILK — BUILDER NUMBER ONE

SEE that the children have all the priority milk they are allowed and that schoolchildren take full advantage of the Milk in Schools Scheme. Let them take their full allowance of milk on their porridge or in puddings or in their mugs, and for the rest of the family use Household Milk for soups and sauces, puddings and cakes. Remember, children should have all their milk, it's just as good for them in puddings as if they drink it fresh.

THE CHILD'S CHEESE RATION

EVERY child over two years should have his full cheese ration. Make cheese scones for tea, give it grated over salad, in sandwiches, or serve it with vegetable soup. Stuff baked potatoes with cheese, and adopt the Danish fashion of serving cheese for breakfast.

THIS IS THE LAST WEEK OF RATION PERIOD No. 4 (Oct. 18th to Nov. 14th)

THE MINISTRY OF FOOD, LONDON, W.1.   FOOD FACTS No. 123

FIVE GOLDEN RULES

1 Give the children their full body-building rations, milk, cheese, eggs, bacon and meat.

2 Give salads and vegetables at the beginning of the meal when the child's appetite is still keen.

3 Avoid fried foods. They are seldom fully digested.

4 Don't let the children have too much starchy food — bread, cereals, puddings, etc. Give these after they've had their body-building foods and vegetables.

5 Don't let the children have pepper, mustard or vinegar — even salt should be used sparingly.

FOOD FACTS

Packed Lunches for a whole week

Six suggestions for a packed meal that are tasty, nourishing and full of variety

Are you stumped to know what to put into the packed lunches your family take off to work ? It *is* a problem.

You don't want to give them the same old thing every day — and it's not good for them, either. People do best on variety, and they need a balance of body-building and energy-giving food, including plenty of protective food, especially greenstuff.

Follow these suggestions. They'll take a load off your mind for a whole week, and they'll make sure the lunches you put up contain proper nourishment.

MONDAY
Sandwiches filled with mixture of cold mashed potato, grated cheese, chutney, and chopped fresh parsley
Lettuce
Jam turnover

TUESDAY
Turnover filled with mixture of chopped cooked beans, melted cheese, and chopped parsley; tomato
Raw cabbage salad in a screw-top jar
Chocolate Pin Wheels

WEDNESDAY
Potato scones filled with scrambled dried eggs, cooked mixed vegetables, and chopped parsley
Watercress
Prune dumplings

THURSDAY
Rissoles made with cooked meat, cooked beans and mashed potato
Raw spinach and lettuce
Fruit turnovers

FRIDAY
Soup
Sandwiches filled with scrambled dried eggs, mashed potato and chopped fried bacon
Radishes or tomatoes
Lettuce

SATURDAY
Turnover filled with sausage meat, cooked dried peas, herbs, parsley, and chopped leek or onion
Raw cabbage salad in a screw-top jar
Oatmeal scones and jam

RATION BOOKS
There is no general re-registration, but you will be able to change a retailer *after August 8th* by applying to the Food Office between August 8th and August 28th. You cannot change your milk retailer.

You may not be able to get all these things where you live, but they are available now in most places. Recipes for any of the above may be had from the Ministry of Food, Portman Square, London, W.1.

THIS IS WEEK 1 — THE FIRST WEEK OF RATION PERIOD No. 1 (July 25th to August 21st)

ISSUED BY THE MINISTRY OF FOOD   FOOD FACTS No. 140

Later in the war, farmers were encouraged to grow cereal crops instead of rearing cattle, since this produced larger quantities of food which was just as nutritious as meat. As a result meat became even more scarce. In 1942 a government survey revealed that over half the workers in heavy industry felt that their meals were inadequate as they were not getting enough meat. It also recorded how people felt about their diet. Here are two of the answers given in reply to the question 'What do you think about wartime food?':

> *Bus Driver (total in family, 6): 'Food not up to standard and not enough of it. Had digestive trouble, which I didn't have before. Potatoes not up to standard. Fish not so fresh.'*
> *Piecer, spinning room (total in family, 2): 'Shops closed when I leave work, so can't get food. Some weeks can't grumble, others can't get anything. Hard work, on feet all day; we're fit for nothing when we get home — we need some decent food.'*
>
> Wartime Social Survey: *Food*, 1942

These replies are typical: the phrase 'not enough' appears again and again in the survey.

Question

What can we learn from this passage about how much food people had in 1942, and how they felt about it? Can you think of any reasons why we should be cautious about accepting what the people said?

The government encouraged the use of all spare land for food crops. Here, men unfit for military service cultivate allotments

Whether or not people liked their new diet, there is little doubt that in some ways it was much better for them. Bread was made from wholemeal flour, and people ate more fresh vegetables and less sugar — in fact they lived on what is now described as a 'high fibre' diet. The government employed nutrition experts to write recipes for the Ministry of Food, so that people could learn how to use their rations sensibly; this meant that for the first time the state began to take control of the nation's nourishment. Rationing was only one aspect of this control.

Subsidised milk was made available to both private and state schools, and by 1945 three-quarters of the nation's children had a regular supply. The system of school meals expanded, too: at the end of the war one child in three ate lunch at school, whereas before the war it was one in 30. Both schemes were taken up by rich and poor alike: the wartime shortages affected everyone equally. From 1940, milk was sold at half price for children and expectant mothers, and there was also a scheme for supplying these groups with cod liver oil and fruit juices.

As a result of the shortages and the new schemes, the diet of the

British citizen undoubtably improved during the war years. Infant mortality dropped; children's teeth were in better condition; the health of old people improved. Rationing ensured that food was fairly distributed, and controls on prices made sure that the scheme worked.

Food policy in the war years was another major advance in the government's involvement in people's welfare. Some historians see it as the starting point of bodies such as the Health Education Authority. Others claim that improved standards of health were just as much the result of other factors, such as high earnings from work in war industries.

In one sense, whether or not it was the result of government action that the nation's health improved was not really important. What did matter was that people had grown used to the government controlling food production, distribution and prices to make sure that there were fair shares for all. After the war some people might object to controls, but it would be hard for any government to reject a system which clearly helped those in need. Once again, peacetime welfare had been created by the pressures of war.

Questions

1 Look closely at the Ministry of Food advertisements and leaflet. Do you think they make the meals they describe sound attractive? Would they have encouraged people to eat them?

2 Talk to your biology or cookery teacher about the nutritional value of these wartime recipes. Compare them with present-day recipes for healthy eating, listing similarities and differences.

The Blitz

Although evacuation and rationing were both important matters, the war touched most people in Britain far more directly. One out of every three houses was damaged in some way, and 220 000 were completely destroyed. Of the 93 000 homes in Hull, for example, only 6000 escaped undamaged. The figures are high, but they do little to convey the suffering, misery and loss: 51 509 civilians were killed in Luftwaffe bombing raids and many times that figure were injured. However, for a long time it had been feared that in the event of war there would be vast numbers of casualties and the government had taken measures to provide some form of medical care for them. In doing so, it laid the foundations for the free hospital service,

Above left: *a rescue party searches for survivors in the ruins of bombed houses in London*
Above right: *a street scene moments after a flying bomb has exploded. Emergency aid was vital for those who were physically unharmed yet deep in shock, but very often it was lacking*

organised in local sectors under overall state control, which was to be a major part of the postwar welfare state.

The organisation was set up as the Emergency Medical Service in 1938. The following year the Civil Defence Act made the Health Ministry responsible for all civilian casualties, and aimed to provide 300 000 beds for them — some 50 000 more than the total number of beds available in peacetime. This target was never reached, but thousands of extra beds were provided, many in wooden huts in hospital grounds. Before the war began, other advances were made as hospitals took advantage of government funds: 1000 new operating theatres were built, a blood transfusion service was organised and an Emergency Public Health Laboratory was set up. An important aspect of these advances was that they showed what a national hospital system might achieve.

Although hospitals were supposed to treat those involved in fighting the war before they dealt with civilian casualties, it soon became impossible to follow this rule. The principle of free hospital treatment for anyone who needed it was created: there could be no going back from it after the war.

When the bombing of London began in earnest, it emphasised social divisions. While the rich could go to air-raid shelters in local shops and restaurants in the West End, the people in the Victorian terraces of the East End had no room in their back yards for the government's corrugated-iron Anderson shelters. Some took rolls of bedding and headed 'up West' to the big stores' shelters, such as the one at Dickins and Jones which could take 700 people who were supplied with cakes, coffee and ice cream. Others sheltered in the capital's underground railway stations. At first the government opposed this, fearing that people would be unwilling to leave the stations, thereby disrupting the transport system and hampering the war effort by their absence from work.

As the Blitz wore on, however, much more was done to help civilians. The tube stations were officially opened to shelterers, who were provided with refreshments and makeshift toilets. The Morrison shelter, a large steel cage with a flat top which doubled as a dining-room table, was sent to houses which had no room for an outdoor shelter. Gradually it was realised that both rich and poor needed proper protection, and in many ways the nation was brought together by the shared suffering of the Blitz and the common purpose of the fighting.

After the Blitz came the bombing of provincial cities. Coventry, Southampton and Plymouth suffered particularly heavy raids, and the Emergency Medical Service was put to the test. Yet there were casualties other than the injured: the shocked, frightened and hungry people whose homes had been destroyed. Some had refused evacuation in 1939; others remained to be near their work. Many of these people had been unemployed or poorly paid in the thirties, and had no savings to fall back on. The government's attitude was clear: such people should 'stay put' and not go to safe areas now, otherwise vital war production would be interrupted and people would lose the will to fight on. Despite this, in many places there was little organisation to help the homeless, as these accounts of people's feelings just after a raid make clear:

Everywhere you go they tell you you can't go there.

It's my belief the Government's brought this on us. And then they don't help you. They all ought to be hung. We'd be better off.

They ought to do something to help. We can't stand any more of this. We'd like to get away but you can't afford to get away for long. They sent us away for a fortnight. But we had to pay 17s. 6d. — you can't pay that and pay your rent too.

Contemporary comments quoted in Tom Harrisson's book,
Living Through the Blitz, 1976

Questions

1   Look carefully at the use of the word 'they' in these passages. To whom do you think it refers? What is the speakers' attitude towards 'them'?

2   What aspects of the government's wartime policy (discussed in this chapter) might have encouraged this attitude? Does this tell us anything about what people now expected from the government in terms of social welfare aid?

The needs of the homeless were great — they required food, shelter, clothing, news of lost relatives, and perhaps above all simple human contact and comfort to offset the dreadful isolation of their suffering.

Practical help was offered by the Assistance Board, which had been given powers to make payments or give other help — an important extension of a body which had been created to give help to the unemployed. After the heavy raids on Plymouth in April 1940, for example, nearly 5000 people were given aid by the Board's local representative, to a total of £70 000. Yet 7000 people received nothing, and in other places even this level of aid was not available. Voluntary bodies such as the Women's Voluntary Service, the Salvation Army and the Young Men's Christian Association were often the only lifeline to those desperately adrift on the tide of war.

Much of the problem was the result of the sheer scale of the suffering. The government had prepared for thousands of dead and injured, but not for thousands of homeless people. Yet there was a feeling that more could have been done. Difficulties were increased by the fact that different problems were dealt with by separate organisations: the Ministry of Health, the Assistance Board, Local Medical Officers, the Billeting Officer and many more. A homeless person might have to visit 15 different organisations simply to continue his or her daily life.

So although the problems that resulted from the bombing raids were very different from those of peacetime, they had one vital thing in common: they were dealt with by many separate organisations which had no contact with each other. At the point where there was greatest need for simple, human warmth, the old system revealed its traditional weakness. This was yet another force in the growing pressure for reform in government welfare provision.

Sacrifice and change

What are we as Members of Parliament to say to the soldiers, the housewives, and the men who are carrying on the services? When they point out the sacrifices and the death and disaster that have taken place in London and in Scotland, England and Wales, are the Government merely to say it is because we are resisting Hitler? Have the Government no reward to offer? The men, the working women and the boys and girls who are making great sacrifices, have a right to ask the Government, 'What is your policy for the future of this country, and what do you guarantee in return for our sufferings?'
J.J. Davidson, MP, *The Parliamentary Debates*,
15 October 1940

This passage shows that even at an early stage of the war the idea of fighting for a better country was being discussed. The sacrifices made by ordinary people were one reason for this; but there were other forces working to secure a better future. One was the presence in Winston Churchill's coalition government of several important

wonder where he is?

Twilight.
The sky is filled with
droning . . . droning . . .
Bombers are going out
— I wonder where he is
"—*my Peter!*"
He too is going out
somewhere —
— now.
Laughing —
yes, laughing of course!
With his boys,
Jock, his gunner,
Dave the Australian,
Poker Face—second
pilot and Shorty —
the imperturbable :
Cup o'cawffee, Sir?
To think,
Last week he was home;
The stories he told
of them. . . . . .
and the old kite—
'Peter's Delivery Van!'
Good luck to them—all.
Baby's asleep, Peter,
Some day—
Some day
You'll come home
for good
May that day be soon.

* * * *

Another form of sacrifice. In advertisements like this one, the public were asked to invest money in National Savings to help the war effort

Labour politicians. Like many people, they remembered the hungry thirties and were determined that such hardship should not occur again.

There was also a strong feeling that, if the government could spend thousands of millions of pounds on fighting a war, it could also spend money to create jobs in peacetime. The idea of the government controlling the nation's industry and economy to make this happen is well summed up in an article which appeared in 1941:

> *Reconstruction must be planned exactly as war production ought to be planned.... Man-power must be controlled so that it can be directed where it is most needed.... In fact, we must have a national plan of reconstruction.*
>
> Thomas Balogh: 'The First Necessity in the New Britain: Work for All', *Picture Post*, 4 January 1941

All these factors led to the setting up, in 1942, of a committee to enquire into government provision of insurance against sickness and unemployment. That same year, *Social Insurance and Allied Services* appeared as a result – the Beveridge Report mentioned in Chapter 1. It accepted that it was the state's responsibility to help the individual through times of hardship, whatever the cause. Beveridge explained the scheme in a radio broadcast:

> *The Security Plan has three sides to it. It includes, first, a scheme of all-in social insurance for cash benefits. It includes, second, a general scheme of children's allowances both when the responsible parent is earning and when he is not earning. It includes, third, an all-in scheme of medical treatment of every kind for everybody.... For the things which everyone needs – pensions in old age, funeral expenses, medical treatment – everyone will be insured. And everyone will be insured for these and all other benefits appropriate to him and his family by a single weekly contribution paid through one insurance stamp.*
>
> William Beveridge: 'Security for All', BBC Home Service broadcast, reprinted in *The Listener*, 10 December 1942

Beveridge's report was very popular. It sold 635 000 copies – a vast figure for a government report, especially in the confusions of wartime life. Workers in mines and factories met to discuss it, and to vote that it should be put into practice straight away. Yet some members of the government were not convinced. They gave the report a limited welcome, rejecting parts of it so that *Picture Post*, a widely-read illustrated weekly, snapped: 'It has filleted it. It has taken out the backbone and bony structure.' Some newspapers, especially the *Daily Sketch* and *The Daily Telegraph*, opposed the report strongly.

What was the reason for this opposition? After all, as Beveridge said, it did not suggest 'giving to everybody something for nothing and without trouble'. The report's opponents said that although it

At a machine-tool factory near London, workers vote that Beveridge's plan be put into practice without delay

was fine in theory, it would not work in practice. In the words of Herbert Wilkins MP, it would 'fasten on the people a burden of taxation which will render inevitable a catastrophe even worse than that of 1931'. Churchill, as war leader, approached the report cautiously, advising ministers to 'be careful not to raise false hopes'.

Questions

1 How did the public react to the Beveridge Report? What do these reactions show about people's interest in national insurance?

2 From your reading of Chapter 2, say why you think the report's opponents thought it would cause taxes to go up.

3 You are a male factory worker aged 55, married with four children, and exempt from military service because of poor health. Write a diary entry for the day on which a works meeting was held to discuss the Beveridge Report, describing your feelings about how the new scheme will change your life.
  Now repeat the exercise as the worker's wife.

When Parliament voted on the Beveridge Report, some Labour MPs, angry at the government's lack of support for it, proposed an amendment that it be implemented at once. The amendment was defeated, but the wartime coalition was shaken. To the public, it suggested that only the Labour Party was in favour of social insurance. This was less than fair. The Conservatives knew how strongly people felt on the subject, and the very next month Churchill wrote that social insurance must be 'an essential part of any postwar scheme of national betterment'. Shortly afterwards, work began on three White Papers. They discussed health care, employment and social insurance, stressing that the state should be fully involved in all three. They were only proposals, but they showed that the government was taking the report seriously and that a new system of welfare could be created at the end of the war.

Question

Each aspect of World War II dealt with in this chapter helped the coming of the welfare state in a particular way. From your reading of these pages, complete the following table, to show how each factor helped pave the way for different features of the new system.

Aspect	Effects
Evacuation	Revealed poverty to more people, and increased pressure for reform.
Rationing Air raids Wartime effort and sacrifice Emergency Medical Service	

As the war drew to a close, it began to seem that Britain's social welfare system was on the verge of complete change. A year after the third White Paper had appeared, the fighting ended at last with the surrender of Japan. Now there was no more war: was there to be no more want?

1945	Family Allowances Act	5s. (25p) per week for every child except the first.
1946	National Insurance Act	26s. (£1.30) for worker / 16s. (80p) for wife / 7s. 6d. (37½p) for child — Benefits for sickness, unemployment and retirement.
1946	National Health Service Act	Free treatment for workers and their dependants by family doctor, dentist, ophthalmologist or as hospital out-patient or in-patient.
1946	National Insurance (Industrial Injury) Act	Injury benefit of 46s. (£2.30) per week for 6 months; Disablement benefit (variable rate); Supplementary benefit; Death benefits for dependants.
1948	Children Act	Children Officers created in local authorities to protect children in care.
1948	National Assistance Act	Benefits for people not covered by other insurance schemes. Run by a National Assistance Board, replacing the old regional Assistance Boards.

Question

Look carefully at the table. Say how the new schemes changed welfare provision in these areas:

a) medical treatment for wives and dependants of working men;
b) allowances for dependants of sick and unemployed men;
c) relationship between sickness and unemployment benefits;
d) pensions for the retired.

THE WELFARE STATE

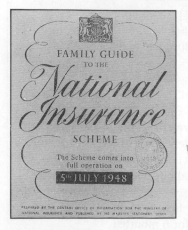

FAMILY GUIDE
TO THE
National Insurance
SCHEME

The Scheme comes into
full operation on
5th JULY 1948

PREPARED BY THE CENTRAL OFFICE OF INFORMATION FOR THE MINISTRY OF
NATIONAL INSURANCE AND PUBLISHED BY HIS MAJESTY'S STATIONERY OFFICE

*How the public learned
about the welfare state: the
Family Guide of 1948*

*Claiming the first week's
family allowance, August
1946*

> *Tomorrow there will come into operation the most comprehensive
> system of social security ever introduced into any country. We may
> be proud that Britain, which has given the lead in so many things to
> the world, is still in the forefront of social advance.*
>
> Clement Attlee: 'The New Social Services and the Citizen',
> BBC Home Service broadcast, 4 July 1948, reprinted in
> *The Listener*, 8 July 1948

When the Labour Party was swept to power under Clement Attlee in
the general election of 1945, it met many problems. The country was
exhausted after the war. Towns were devastated; those people who
were physically unhurt were suffering from bereavement and loss;
rationing of food and other essential goods had to be continued
because of shortages; and only through massive exports could Britain
pay its way. Yet despite all this, there was hope. This was the
people's government, pledged to build a new society – the people's
peace after the people's war. The feature of the new Britain which
most affected people's lives was the group of Acts (see page 47)
creating what became known as the welfare state.

The Family Allowances Act had been passed by Churchill's coalition in 1945, and the first allowances were paid in August 1946. Four
of the other Acts came into force on 5 July 1948 – the 'Appointed

Day'. Attlee's broadcast to the nation on the eve of that day began with the words quoted above and went on to explain the new measures:

First, these four schemes are part of a general plan, and they fit in with each other. Secondly, they are not designed to meet the needs of a particular section of the community. They are comprehensive and available to every citizen. They give security to all the members of the family. Thirdly, a word about the method of payment: National Assistance, like Family Allowances, will be paid for entirely by the Exchequer, that is to say, you do not pay for them directly but through the taxes to which we all contribute. The National Health Service will be paid for mainly by the Exchequer. The other services are insurance services, paid for by direct contributions from those who are insured, and from their employers, if they are employed, with assistance from the state out of general taxation. You pay your contribution towards the benefits to which you and your family are entitled, by sticking a single stamp on a card each week.

Questions

1 Why is it important that the schemes are 'part of a general plan'?

2 How does the fact that the schemes were 'available to every citizen' make them different from earlier welfare services? Give detailed examples in your answer.

The benefits explained: part of the Family Guide

A married woman who contributes will, if qualified, be able to draw Sickness and Unemployment Benefit, even though her husband is working, but at special rates.

A married woman contributor will also be able to qualify for Retirement Pension from the age of 60 at the full rate of 26s. a week, whether her husband is retired or not.

Married women in Class 1 employment will be compulsorily insured for Industrial Injury, even though they choose not to insure for other benefits.

It is essential that all insured women who marry, and all women who become widows on or after 5th July 1948, should at once notify their local National Insurance Office.

PART THREE

National Insurance Benefits Explained

This Part and Part Four give more information about the individual benefits and the conditions on which they are paid. Some detail, and special conditions affecting comparatively few claims, have been left out. In case of doubt always consult your National Insurance Office.

SICKNESS BENEFIT

20. What are the Rates of Benefit? The standard weekly rate for a man or woman over 18 years of age (except a married woman) is 26s. with an increase of 16s. for an adult dependant and 7s. 6d. for the first child under school leaving age. Children, after the first, will be covered by the Family Allowances Scheme.

... make your claim in good time' ...

The weekly rate for a boy or girl under 18 is 15s., but any boy or girl who is entitled to an increase for an adult dependant or a child will be paid the adult rate.

The weekly rate for an insured married woman is 16s., but she will be paid at the 26s. rate if she has an invalid husband, or cannot get financial support from her husband.

Benefit is not payable for Sundays.

Lower rates of benefit may be paid if you are in hospital for some time.

21. What are the Contribution Conditions? To qualify for any Sickness Benefit you must have paid 26 Class 1 or Class 2 contributions at some time. The standard rate of benefit is payable during a benefit year if in the previous contribution year you paid or have had credited at least 50 Class 1 or Class 2 contributions. If less than 50 have been paid or credited, benefit may still be payable, but at a reduced rate. Until you have paid 156 Class 1 or Class 2 contributions you cannot get Sickness Benefit for more than 312 days (that is, one year not counting Sundays).

Organising the scheme had taken massive effort. Up to the last minute, the British Medical Association – representing GPs and hospital doctors – had rejected the change. They felt that doctors would lose their professional freedom if they worked for the state, and thought the 16s. a year they were paid for each patient was not enough. One doctor expressed a common middle-class fear of Socialism by calling the scheme 'the first step, and a big one, towards National Socialism as practised in Germany'. But at the final stage the health minister, Aneurin Bevan, allowed doctors to keep their private patients, and encouraged the public to register with doctors under the new scheme. Doctors who refused to take Health Service patients would lose income: by the Appointed Day 90 per cent of the doctors had joined the scheme.

Great changes were made in the way the national insurance scheme was run. New headquarters were built in Newcastle so that the Civil Service could take over the work previously done by the friendly societies. The offices covered 64 acres and housed the records of 25 million people – including 600 000 Smiths – in 100 rooms. The Ministry planned to open 1000 local offices throughout the nation, where claims would be settled; by the Appointed Day 912 offices were in operation with a staff of 17 000.

Massive publicity was given to the scheme. An employer's guide was sent to 100 000 employers, a film was made, and a series of posters displayed. Forty-eight leaflets were written and a total of 50 million copies were printed. Most important was the leaflet which dropped through the letterboxes of 14 million homes. Called *The Family Guide to the National Insurance Scheme*, it set out the plan in simple, clear language.

Part of the national insurance records office at Newcastle

A local national insurance office. In the first year ten million claims were made and 42 million weekly payments were issued throughout the country

On 5 July 1948 *The Times* summed up the nation's mood:

> *In the maze and jumble of 'post-war reconstruction' as it actually is, it would be a grave mistake to overlook the deep feelings and sense of purpose and common humanity which all the new social services are trying, however imperfectly, to express.*

It was a time of expectation and hope: would the new service really change people's lives?

'Also, I need not have lost my baby...'

> *I think it's wonderful, one of the finest things that ever happened in this country. For the first time it isn't a matter of a person's bank balance which decides whether he's going to live or die. In the past there's many a man had to think twice before seeing a doctor, even if he was very ill. You can appreciate what it must have meant to thousands from the stories you hear of crowded doctors' surgeries and queues for spectacles.*
>
> Woman metal polisher, aged 50, quoted in Tom Harrisson and Charles Madge's book, *Meet Yourself at the Doctor's*, 1949

Despite appeals from officials not to expect 'everything at once' from the new system, it seems clear that this statement sums up the feeling of many on the Appointed Day. All branches of the new Health Service were used heavily. Between July and September 1948, 36 million prescriptions were dispensed; before the new service, the monthly average had been seven million. By October 1949, eight and a quarter million people had been prescribed spectacles, and eight and a half million had been treated by a dentist. Some visits to the doctor were 'unjustifiable, even frivolous', in the words of the Ministry

51

of Health report. But perhaps only a trained doctor could judge the truth of this; for many people such visits must have been a source of comfort.

The new service probably had most effect on the lives of married women who were not working. For the first time, they and their children were covered for treatment under their husbands' contributions. This was a considerable difference from the earlier scheme.

You can bring the children to the surgery and get attended there free. Sometimes when Aggie [little girl] was sick, I usedn't to have the money when he came. It's everything to a mother to know that you can call the doctor even when you haven't the money — you have to count it day by day just how you spend it. And if you go to the Children's Hospital, you have to spend hours and hours waiting. It's awkward taking Aggie up to the Children's Hospital, same as I have done, and the little boy coming in from school for his dinner.

Wife of crane-driver, aged 34, quoted in *Meet Yourself at the Doctor's*, as above

Before the NHS, few people could afford to visit an optician. Instead, they bought spectacles at Woolworth's:

Stacked on the counter were spectacles, with a large card with a large A going down to a small Z.... I can see my father now, trying on different pairs of glasses, looking at the card, putting down a pair, picking another pair up, until he got the selected pair.... I'd say 'You look smashing, Dad,' and then we'd just go out of the store.

Mr Law quoted in Paul Addison's book, *Now the War is Over*, 1985

Above left: *the old system: queuing for the doctor at a public hospital, 1939*
Above right: *...and the new system: the surgery of Dr Killick, Williton, Somerset, 1948. How is it different from the hospital surgery?*

Now, things were different. Mrs Clare Bond describes her sister's experience:

...as soon as the NHS started, she was there, [at the] optician. Marvellous NHS spectacles, you know, some style about them. So she didn't hesitate at wearing glasses any more after that.

Quoted in *Now the War is Over*, as above

The Ministry report reached this conclusion:

It is clear that many elderly people who had not had their sight tested previously, although they had obtained spectacles by some such method of purchase or inheritance, immediately took advantage of this provision which they needed.

Report of the Ministry of Health, 1949, 1950

How did the doctors respond to the change? One thought the fees 'disgustingly inadequate' and found he had 'practically no time at all left for any private life'. He went on to object to the amount of record-keeping:

It's all paper-work — I'm inundated with it. Look at these. I'm sending patients to hospital, so I've got to fill these damn things in. It's senseless. And all for sixteen bob a year.

'Dr Y', quoted in *Meet Yourself at the Doctor's*, as above

Another doctor was more positive:

A male district nurse visits a patient's home, 1949

I very much like not having to send out all those wretched bills. I like to feel I don't have to worry about making an extra call if I think it is necessary. In the old days there was always the thought that patients might feel I was trying to get an extra seven-and-six out of them...there seem to be far more women patients than there used to be, prior to N.H.S., and I think the main reason is that many women simply wouldn't think of calling in a doctor unless they were absolutely prostrated, largely because of the expense. Now that they have the N.H.S. they tend to visit the doctor as soon as possible, and whilst it may mean more immediate work for the doctor, it probably prevents serious conditions developing in many cases which would finally entail far more work.

'Dr D', quoted in *Meet Yourself at the Doctor's*, as above

For some, however, the changes came too late. The following passages show the difference between the old and new medicine, and the suffering which the NHS was intended to prevent:

[The new system] benefited me mentally, because for many years we suffered terrible privation through having to pay doctors' and chemists' bills. At last we had to sell house and most of home. Also, I need not have lost my baby. I had to go out to work to earn the fees as well as nurse a sick husband.

Teacher, quoted in *Meet Yourself at the Doctor's*, as above

Inside a local insurance office. Is this the 'discriminating, humane administration' promised by the Minister of Health?

Dad thought it was wonderful, because he...had a small wage, and thought with a family of four children to bring up, it was just too much for him to be able to go to the doctor.... He used to buy some concoction from the chemist at sixpence a bottle, that eased his pains in his stomach. But when he went on the National Health Service, this was thoroughly investigated, and they found out that Dad hadn't a stomach upset, Dad had cancer. Had it been treated earlier, [it] could have been cured but unfortunately, due to the expensive doctors, Dad had not had this looked into before, and we lost Dad, Dad died of cancer.

Mrs Clare Bond, quoted in *Now the War is Over*, as above

Questions

1   Make a list of the ways in which the NHS changed the lives of working people. Include as many aspects as you can, covering both treatment of illness and larger changes in people's lives.

2   How did the new system affect the lives of married women? Support your answer with references to the people quoted above.

3   It is the evening of 5 July 1948. You are a GP in a busy practice in an industrial town. Write a diary entry recording the events of the day, mentioning the patients you have seen, their attitudes to the new scheme, and your own feelings about the new system and what it will achieve.

Rebuilding Britain

Whole quarters of towns were almost destroyed, and there was a passionate determination to rebuild them and rebuild them better which led the Government to undertake that after the war there should be finer towns and a more prosperous countryside in Britain.

HMSO: *Town and Country Planning 1943–1951*, 1951

Even during the war years, the importance of building a better Britain was not forgotten. A series of reports discussed the planning of industrial and housing development, the problem of fair compensation for those whose land was bought by the government, and the serious 'drift from the land' – the movement of people from the country to the cities. At the height of the V-2 raids on the capital, the *Greater London Plan* was published. It called for 'new towns' outside London, the control of industrial building, a 'green belt' of fields around the capital to stop the growth of suburban housing and to provide recreation for Londoners. It was not only what it said that showed how important the subject was to the government, but how it said it: the report was a large, hardback volume, with scores of glossy illustrations and – unlike any other wartime government publication – colour plates.

Before these ideals could be put into practice, however, there was the crying need of the homeless to be considered. One rapid solution was prefabrication – building whole sections of houses on factory production lines, so that they could be easily and quickly assembled on site. Between the end of the war and 1948, 124 455 such houses were built, the most common being the aluminium bungalows known as 'prefabs'. Made on production lines which only months before had been making heavy bombers, they offered built-in cookers, kitchen fitments and bathrooms of a high standard. Many remained in use for over 20 years, and even in the late 1980s some are still occupied in parts of London.

Successful though they were, 'prefabs' and the other temporary houses were designed to be only a short-term solution to the housing crisis. People who could not find homes were reduced to 'squatting' in empty army camps or deserted houses. Many were angry: where was the new Jerusalem the government had promised? Shortages of materials had delayed the building of the new communities outlined by the *Greater London Plan*, but there was no shortage of ideas. For the first time, the way the land was used was to be controlled. According to the Town and Country Planning Act of 1947, there was to be 'a framework, or pattern, of land use', instead of the haphazard growth of the thirties. A more significant expression of this idea was the New Towns Act of 1946, which had given the Ministry authority to 'designate' areas where whole new communities could be created.

The idea of planning a whole new town had been put into practice many years before in private schemes such as Letchworth Garden City. The New Towns Act added government authority to these schemes. Towns were to be built in open countryside and designed as self-contained communities. Each would be divided into 'zones' for industry, shopping, housing and recreation. People would live and work in the same community, and houses would be built to the highest standards.

Realising that the most important part of any town was its people, the New Towns Committee tried hard to avoid a problem which had always existed in towns: the separation of people into groups according to their income. Instead of such separation, the Committee wanted towns which were 'truly balanced' communities.

How did this work in practice? Stevenage, the first new town, was designated in 1947, and there were 12 in all by 1950. Many, such as Harlow, Hemel Hempstead and Crawley, were sited near London for those made homeless by bombing or slum clearance. Others, such as Aycliffe and Peterlee, catered for the needs of people in the north of England. A very high proportion of the inhabitants of new towns

A 'prefab' still in use in 1970, in Tower Hamlets, London

were young married couples. Was it possible to create a community almost overnight in which people could really feel at home? Ben Hyde Harvey, finance officer at Harlow when the first people moved in, called the town a 'marvellous place to be, because of the frontier spirit'. He went on:

> It was truly that in the first years. Harlow was a prairie of mud, the prams were like covered wagons drawn up around the few shops. But the people were super. We were building them this green city they have now — it was going to be a marvellous place to bring up their kids, so they endured. And they contributed. They made their own entertainment, shared their interests!
> ... We didn't want houses for grannies at first. We gave in and it became one of the best things we ever did... fitting in those little blocks on the corners imported not only baby-sitters and part-time workers for the community, it imported wisdom.
>
> Quoted in Brian James's article, 'How fares the Brave New Town?', *The Times*, 13 March 1987

After the suffering of war, the new towns must have seemed 'marvellous' to their first inhabitants. But what were they like to live in once the novelty had worn off? In 1977 a reporter visited Harlow to see how it looked after 30 years. He found a poor transport system, and a population more working-class than classless. Many of the inhabitants commuted daily to London, the town centre had 'dreary down-market shops' and was 'like a morgue at night'. But the residents were happy:

> It's a great place to bring the kids. So much grass and green....

> I enjoy it tremendously. There is stacks to do, and the council is tremendously good. They really look after the elderly.
>
> Quoted in Roger Berthoud's article, 'Harlow 30 years after: how the dream stands up to reality', *The Times*, 16 December 1977

Questions

1   Explain what Ben Hyde Harvey meant by 'the frontier spirit'. How do you think this spirit helped the first inhabitants of Harlow?

2   What do you think he meant when he described the 'grannies' as 'part-time workers for the community'? How did they bring 'wisdom' to the new town?

3   You are a married woman with two children under five. Three months ago you moved to Harlow from a crowded, bomb-damaged street in London's East End. Describe how the way you live in the new town compares with what you had expected of it.

WELFARE AFTER BEVERIDGE

We were very idealistic at the time, because we were brainwashed into thinking that the Health Service would be so wonderful that everybody would be much fitter, all serious diseases would be cured and there was a danger that in a few years' time doctors might become redundant because there'd be insufficient work for them.

Dr G. Jaffe, quoted in Paul Addison's book, *Now the War is Over*, 1985

Question

Why does the writer use the word 'brainwashed' here? What does this reveal about attitudes towards the Health Service when it was created?

The coming of the welfare state was greeted with delight and relief, and the hope that Beveridge's giants would indeed be slain. In some areas, the early hopes were fulfilled. With postwar unemployment at less than a quarter of a million, benefit payments were few, and the unemployment fund actually had a surplus of £95 million at the end of its first year.

There was no such security for the medical service. Some departments simply could not cope with the demand. Opticians were one example; dentists were another. There were delays, and an emergency

The new dental service came under severe pressure in the fifties

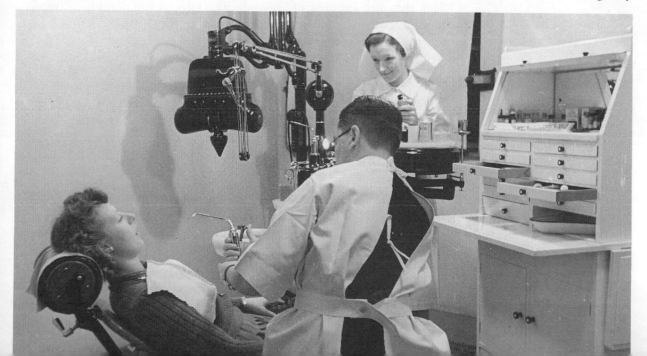

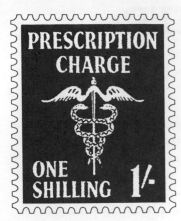

The end of welfare? A prescription stamp, used to pay the new charge in 1952

'relief from pain' dental service had to be set up. Ambulances were in short supply, and many were worn-out vehicles that had been in use before the war.

The biggest difficulties were with the hospital service. It was still essentially the same as before the war, although the Emergency Medical Service had united the municipal and voluntary systems and increased the number of beds available so that there were just over half a million on the Appointed Day. But buildings were old: 45 per cent had been built before 1891 and 24 per cent before 1861. Shortages of materials meant that no new hospitals had been built since 1939.

Meanwhile, costs soared. Estimates for the first year of the NHS had given a total cost of £170 million; in reality it was £242 million.

A turning point came in 1951. With Britain's involvement in the Korean War making demands on the Exchequer, the Chancellor, Hugh Gaitskell, introduced charges for dentures and spectacles, to the outrage of Bevan, who resigned from the Ministry of Health. The same year, the Conservatives were returned to power, to remain there for 13 years. They believed that only those who could not afford drugs should have them free, and that others should pay a contribution towards the cost. In 1952, charges were imposed on all prescriptions, and the age of free medicine for all was over.

The new affluence

By the 1950s it was clear that society had changed. The postwar 'baby boom' had produced a million more children, adding to the pressure on medical care and lengthening the bill for family allowances. There were also another million and a half pensioners. It was clear that the funding of the welfare state, if not its whole nature, must change too. A contemporary analyst posed the question which was to dominate welfare policy from then on:

> *Whether or not we as a nation are to cling sentimentally to the label of 'welfare state', we have to accept some of the economic burden of these additional children and some part of the heavier burden of old age. The question is: how shall these burdens be distributed along with the existing costs of the social services?*
>
> R.M. Titmuss: 'Crisis in the Social Services', *The Listener*, 14 February 1952

The answer favoured by the Conservatives was contained in one word: 'selectivity'. Welfare benefits should be made available only to those in genuine need, and those who could afford to be independent of the state must be urged to do so. Writing in 1960, Geoffrey Howe urged that 'over the whole field of social policy our firm aim should ...be a reduction in the role of the state'. Partly as a result, the old policy of equal contributions and benefits for all was abandoned. In 1959 a graduated pension scheme was introduced in which workers paid larger contributions, to secure larger benefits, if they earned above a specified amount. In 1962 graduated national insurance contributions were introduced on the same principle.

In the fifties, the decade that saw the beginning of the 'affluent society', living standards rose rapidly for many working people. Cars, televisions, household electrical goods and regular holidays all became familiar features of life. In the face of such affluence it was easy to think that poverty had vanished with the ration books: yet this was far from true.

In 1960 the sociologist Professor Peter Townsend estimated that seven per cent of all families, including two and a quarter million children, were living in poverty. At the same time the whole question of what poverty meant came under investigation. Rowntree had defined it according to the ability of an individual to supply his or her basic needs. In the sixties, however, there were different views, expressed most clearly in an influential article:

> *Poverty is not an absolute state. It is relative deprivation. Society is itself continually changing and thrusting new obligations on its members. They, in turn, develop new needs. . . .*
>
> *Our general theory, then, should be that individuals and families whose resources, over time, fall seriously short of the resources commanded by the average individual or family in the community in which they live, whether that community is a local, national or international one, are in poverty.*
>
> Peter Townsend: 'The Meaning of Poverty', *British Journal of Sociology*, October 1962

Questions

1 Explain Townsend's definition of poverty in your own words. How is it different from earlier definitions?

2 In small groups, discuss what you understand by 'poverty'. Give some examples of the items which most people have, and without which someone might be thought 'poor'. How might your definition of poverty differ if you lived in a Third World country?

In 1966, A.B. Atkinson published the results of research which estimated that five million people lived in poverty. The same year, the Supplementary Benefits Commission was created, to decide on the amounts of money to be paid to the poor. It was now called supplementary benefit instead of national assistance. Aid of this kind seemed to carry with it the disgrace of the old Poor Law relief, since many people, especially the elderly — 700 000 in one survey — did not claim benefits to which they were entitled because of pride or a desire to be independent. In 1968 the Seebohm Report appeared, urging that more money should be spent on caring for 'problem families' by improving their housing, income and general standard of living. It was clear that, although many people were enjoying affluence and financial security, a significant proportion of the population was suffering hardship.

Seebohm linked social problems with bad housing, as Rowntree had done many years before. Certainly, housing became a major problem in the 1960s. The previous decade had seen a record amount of building, with 300 000 homes begun in 1952–3 under Harold Macmillan. The boom in property development in the sixties meant that land prices soared, and many local authorities built high-rise flats — tower blocks intended to solve the housing crisis overnight. They did not. Those built from prefabricated sections were unsafe; in the late sixties a gas explosion tore apart a block of flats at Ronan Point in London, and the inquiry that followed blamed the method of construction. Those that were soundly built created many problems for their tenants. Electric heating was far too expensive to use; the elderly found it impossible to climb countless stairs when the lifts were out of order or vandalised; and, though play areas were often provided, few parents were happy to leave children to play unsupervised 12 storeys beneath them. Most of all, there was no sense of community; high-rise tenants missed the friendship of the terrace with its pub at one end and shop at the other. As Anthony Quiney remarked in a recent history of housing: 'It is hard to get on with neighbours you hear overhead but never see next door.'

Below left: *building the new Britain: a mechanical lift speeding up roofing in 1950*
Below right: *it seemed a good idea . . . high density housing and its designer*

Today and tomorrow

Since the sixties, problems have crowded in on the welfare state. The soaring inflation of the early seventies, and the need for pensions to keep pace with it, has imposed heavy burdens on the pension scheme. Beveridge's plan for the unemployment insurance fund assumed a maximum rate of 3½ per cent jobless, but in the eighties the figure has never been below three times that level. In the seventies, governments of both parties were forced to cut welfare spending. Population changes have caused further difficulties: research carried out by Rudolf Klein and John Ashley in 1972 suggested that by 1992 three-quarters of the hospital beds for men and 93.7 per cent of those for women will be occupied by pensioners. The AIDS epidemic will impose immense strains on a system already under-equipped for the care of the terminally ill. While the suburbs prosper, the inner cities decay, and homelessness among people of all ages is on the increase.

The Conservative government under Margaret Thatcher has, since 1979, sought to counter these problems by lowering taxes, in the hope that this will encourage people to work harder, create new jobs and thus increase the nation's wealth. Private medical insurance has grown, and investment of all kinds now makes possible better provision for retirement. Yet critics say that, like the old *laissez-faire* system, these policies help the young and affluent and not those in real need. A wide range of job creation and training schemes has helped young unemployed people and those made redundant by industrial decline. Opponents of these say that they offer no hope of permanent employment, and that the money they cost would be better spent on building roads, houses and hospitals to create jobs

A new private hospital, one of many begun in the eighties

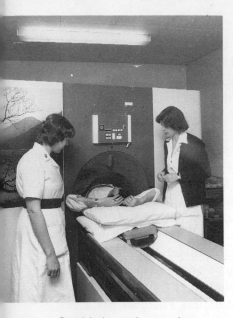

Sophisticated scanning equipment in use at a National Health Service hospital

and improve the nation's welfare. For those people who have bought their own council houses under legislation of the early eighties, the new scheme is a move towards greater personal security. But for the growing numbers on council waiting lists there is little hope, with the number of new houses built falling from 176 000 in 1976 to a mere 39 100 in 1985.

The situation today is full of contradictions. Local authorities cannot afford to build houses to rent, yet have to pay for homeless people to stay in hotels for 'bed and breakfast'. Such accommodation for a family might, in a year, cost as much as building a new council flat. Preventive medicine, which tries to keep people healthy, has been introduced, with 'well woman clinics' and special care of the elderly. Yet doctors in inner cities work from run-down shops which they keep padlocked for fear of theft. Intensive care and advanced surgery are as sophisticated in Britain as anywhere else in the world; yet in many areas people have to wait one or even two years for simple operations. Family income supplement, which replaced supplementary benefit in 1971, pays out millions of pounds to low-paid workers; yet pharmacists report that many people collect only one item on a prescription as they cannot afford to pay for two or three.

Key issues have affected the welfare state from the very beginning. Should it be financed by contributions from workers or by grants from the Exchequer? Should it be available for everyone or only those in need? And how do we decide who is to pay and who is to receive free treatment and welfare benefits? Alongside these issues of principle have been practical problems. How do you organise a system that is quick and efficient, yet still treats people with kindness and understanding? How do you balance the demands of medicine and national insurance against those of housing, education, overseas aid and all the other items of government spending?

While the debate continues, those at the lowest level of subsistence fall further behind those who enjoy adequate incomes. Early in 1987, a newspaper article described life on a local authority housing estate in an area of high unemployment. It shows clearly the problems of

1980s: unemployment is very high, especially among young black people

those trying to keep going with some dignity in a period which has already been called 'the post-welfare state':

> *The house is in a bad state: the lavatory is disconnected, the plaster has come away from the wall exposing the brick beneath; the back door doesn't fit....*
>
> *Winnie has always collected little ornaments: the shelves around the walls are full of glass animals, brass and porcelain. The visitor from Social Security told her she should sell them before asking for any more public money....*
>
> *Winnie lifts up her thick cardigan to show the wasting flesh of her stomach. 'We're starving, cock,' she says. Without conscious irony, she taps her packet of cigarettes. 'These are the only thing that are keeping me alive.'*

Jeremy Seabrook: 'Survivors on the welfare estate',
The Independent, 17 January 1987

A team of workers on a Manpower Services scheme to restore a trolley-bus as a museum exhibit

Questions

1 List the similarities and the differences between this passage and those from the *Memoirs of the Unemployed* on pages 30–31. For example, do you think that there is still a sense of disgrace in being poor, or is today's system more compassionate? Then discuss your answers in small groups.

2 Listed below are some problems facing welfare provision in Britain. In small groups, discuss possible solutions to them.
   a) Paying unemployment benefit for long periods to large numbers of people.
   b) Financing the NHS.
   c) Providing pensions and enough medical facilities for the growing number of elderly people.
   d) Deciding who is to receive help if a selective NHS system were to be introduced.

New dawn or final sunset? Children play on the Ryecroft estate, Walsall

INDEX

Numerals in **bold** denote
illustrations